LEADERS IN ACTION SERIES BOOK TWO

BIBLICAL LEADERSHIP IN TURBULENT TIMES

LESSONS LEARNED FROM GOOD BIBLICAL LEADERS

GREGORY E. VON TOBEL

MAHANAIM CREEK PUBLISHERS LLC
WOODINVILLE, WASHINGTON

ISBN: 9798698169352

Library of Congress Control Number: 2020920511

Other books by Gregory E. Von Tobel

Personal

Staving Off Disaster- A Journey in Spiritual Fasting

Biblical Leadership in Turbulent Times- Book 1- Basic Leadership Principles for Christian Leaders

Prison Ministry- Basic Training

Prison Ministry Training- Part 1- Getting Started

Prison Ministry Training- Part 2- Volunteer Recruiting, Training and Oversight

Prison Ministry Training- Part 3- Conducting an Effective Bible Study, Church Service, Altar Call, Prison Ministry Network, and Working with Staff

This book is dedicated to the Lord Jesus Christ my Lord and Savior,

To my dearest wife, Rhonda, who encourages me and allows me to write,

And to all that come behind us laboring in the jails and prisons of the world.

CONTENTS

CHAPTER 1

JOSEPH - A MAN OF ADMINISTRATION

Joseph had a rough start with family. Though he was dearly loved by his father and mother, Rachel and Jacob, this was not the case with his ten older brothers. Joseph, the youngest of the ten, was arrogant and—to use today's language—a young punk. Genesis 37:4 states, "When his brothers saw that their father loved him more than any of them, they hated him and could not speak a kind word to him." Because of the favoritism shown by his father and Joseph's own youthful pride, there was enmity between him and his brothers.

We first learn of Joseph in Genesis 37 when he is seventeen years old. The Bible describes an incident when Joseph brought his father a bad report about his brothers while they were tending the family flocks. Unsurprisingly, Joseph's tattling angered his brothers. More trouble was on the horizon. The Bible next describes Joseph recounting one of his own dreams to his brothers. In the dream, all the brothers were gathering sheaves in the field, while Joseph's sheaf stood upright, all of their sheaves were bowing down to his sheaf. This recounting of the dream infuriated his brothers as they correctly interpreted the dream to mean that they would one day have to bow down to their younger brother.

Their fury, consequently, developed into jealousy, which later turned into a murder plot.

If not for their oldest brother, Reuben, the brothers' murderous plot may well have ended with Joseph's death. At Reuben's bidding, the brothers reconsidered killing Joseph. Instead they sold him to a caravan of Ishmaelites who were traveling to Egypt. Not having the courage to tell their father they had sold his beloved son into slavery, the brothers then concocted a lie. They took Joseph's brightly-colored robe—a lavish gift from his father which they had stripped off Joseph before selling him—and dipped it in blood, convincing Jacob that Joseph had been killed by a wild animal instead.

Meanwhile, the Ishmaelites had taken Joseph to Egypt and had sold him to Potiphar, the captain of the guard, which—presumably—was a high position in Egypt. It is further presumed that Potiphar had been appointed by Pharaoh, who bestowed Potiphar with wealth, a prominent position within the country, and even an audience with Pharaoh himself. The Bible adds that Potiphar had jurisdiction over the prisons and certainly over all the executioners in the land, making it likely that Potiphar even had the power to put Joseph to death, though he never did. The Bible describes Joseph's tenure with his master in verses 39:2-6.

> The LORD was with Joseph and he prospered, and he lived in the house of his Egyptian master. When his master saw that the LORD was with him and that the Lord gave him success in everything he did, Joseph found favor in his eyes and became his attendant. Potiphar put him in charge of his household, and he entrusted to his care everything he owned. From the time he put him in charge of his

household and of all that he owned, the LORD blessed the household of the Egyptian because of Joseph. The blessing of the LORD was on everything Potiphar had, both in the house and in the field. So, he left Joseph's care everything he had; with Joseph in charge, he did not concern himself with anything except the food he ate (Gen 39:2-6).

These verses emphasize the great trust Potiphar placed in Joseph. Despite this trust, though, calamity once again pursued Joseph when he was falsely accused of sexual improprieties by Potiphar's wife. After these accusations, Potiphar had no other recourse but to throw Joseph into one of his prisons. Once again, Joseph lost his position in life and ended up in a dungeon. Read what the Bible says about his time in prison:

But while Joseph was there in the prison, the LORD was with him; he showed him kindness and granted him favor in the eyes of the prison warden. So, the warden put Joseph in charge of all those held in the prison, and he was made responsible for all that was done there. The warden paid no attention to anything under Joseph's care, because the LORD was with Joseph and gave him success in whatever he did (Gen 39:20-23).

Several passages later, we read that—by the providence of God—the tides once again turned for Joseph, when he was asked to interpret one of Pharaoh's dreams. Pharaoh was so pleased with Joseph's ability to do this that he soon entrusted him with the entire kingdom. Verses 41:41-43 says,

So, Pharaoh said to Joseph, "I hereby put you in charge of the whole land of Egypt." Then Pharaoh took his signet ring from his finger and put it on Joseph's finger. He dressed him in robes of fine linen and put a gold chain around his neck. He had him ride in a chariot as his second-in-command, and men shouted before him, "Make way!" Thus, he put him in charge of the whole land of Egypt.

What can we learn from the life of Joseph?

Joseph went from being the favorite son of his father, to being sold into slavery, to being the head of a high ranking government official's household, to being a prisoner in a dungeon, to being in charge of the entire prison, to being in charge of an entire country. How did all that happen? No human could have orchestrated such great events.

Leadership Life Principle #1: Always seek God's favor in your life. This is truly a story where we see God's favor shown in one man's life. The point here is that when you are bestowed with God's favor, He works on your behalf. Throughout this story we read that "the LORD was with Joseph" and that "the LORD gave him success." Joseph was so successful with what he did that those above him had little to worry about while Joseph was in charge. This is trust in the truest sense, and the magnitude of this kind of trust cannot happen overnight.

I have several people in my life whom I trust impeccably. I also make sure that I acknowledge and reaffirm my trust in them repeatedly. There are several ways I do this: when I assign a task to them, I trust they will perform those duties ethically and to the best of their abilities. On those rare occasions when issues arise and they don't know the best course of action, I also know they will come to me for counsel. Because I trust these individuals completely, they have access to my passwords, pertinent personal information, and even have my permission to sign for me. Do you have such trustworthy people in your life? Have you placed your trust in someone else? This kind of trust is an example of man showing favor toward another person.

But what about God's favor? Is it wrong to pray for God's favor? Absolutely not! In fact, I pray for God's favor relentlessly. I yearn for it in my leadership role and pray that the Lord will proceed before me and be my rear guard, much like He had for Joseph. The Bible gives countless other examples of people in the Bible who were facing insurmountable odds when they sought God's favor.

Leadership Life Principle #2: Learn to be proven faithful in the little things of life. This is certainly a biblical principle. Joseph wasn't promoted overnight to the head of Potiphar's household. He was watched. He was observed. He was tested. As this was taking place, his responsibilities grew. It was the same during his stay in prison. Perhaps his reputation as head of Potiphar's household preceded him to prison. Still, because he was in a new environment, he was watched, observed, and tested before he was put into a position of authority.

If you want to move up in an organization, you first need to be tested and proven. Lazy people do not get promoted. Inefficient people do not get promoted. Unorganized people who let deadlines fall through the cracks do not get promoted. Only people who excel in those areas will be promoted.

Leadership Life Principle #3: Endeavor to grow in your administrative giftedness. The principles of administration have not changed in over five thousand years. Administration today is really no different than it was in the days of the Pharaohs, meaning that even back then, Joseph needed to be organized. This is because monies still needed to be accounted for correctly, things still needed to be put in the right place, and crops still needed to be planted at the right time, harvested at the right time, and properly stored. Furthermore, for Joseph, his servants needed to be managed, fed and business and agricultural cycles still had to be forecasted. Some scholars even believe that because of Joseph's stature in Egypt, he probably even oversaw the military as well. The point is this—all of these procedures needed to be written down, taught to others, and enforced, and these were all part of Joseph's job.

Granted, today we have radically different methods of tracking data than the Egyptians had—with our Excel spreadsheets, databases, and cloud computing; nevertheless, the foundational management principles are still the same.

Only thirteen years had passed between the time Joseph tended to the flocks and the time he became second-in-command of Egypt. Within that short span of thirteen years—and by the grace of God—he had proven himself an excellent administrator. Joseph had gone from slave to second-in-command within those thirteen years. He had learned how to effectively organize and carry out all his responsibilities. If you want to be an extremely effective leader, then you need to excel in your area of administrative giftedness and not be afraid of paperwork. So ask yourself, how well do you do in this area? Are you a stacker? Do you have stacks and stacks of papers mounted high on your desk? Do you have a system of organizing your day? Do you lose paperwork or details frequently? Do you forget appointments? If that's you, and if you are a boss with the ability to hire someone for a managerial or overseer role, make sure you focus on your candidates' abilities to stay organized.

Leadership Life Principle #4: Learn to stay organized. Though a good deal of our "paperwork" is now electronic, we are still a paper-and-application-driven society. For those who are terrified of paperwork and forms, staying on top of the details of life can seem a daunting task. The technical term for this fear of paperwork is *papyrophobia*. Those who have it often struggle with tracking details, causing them to miss deadlines and leave tasks unfinished. Their lives are typically a mess.

If you aspire to be a great leader, it is extremely helpful if you are already gifted with the ability to administrate. If you are not gifted in that area, it does not mean you have little hope of ever being a great leader. It just means that you will need to surround yourself with those who do excel in administration, so that they can fill in the gaps where you are lacking. I know several leaders who are a complete wreck at administration, but who are great leaders nonetheless because they have people around them to assist their weak spots.

What can you do to improve in administration?

1. **Pray daily for God's favor.** Like the persistent widow asking the judge for justice in Luke 18, continue to persist in prayer before the Almighty. Ask for His favor to fall fresh on you daily. Pray that He will teach you how to administrate. Ask Him to bring people or systems into your life who can help you stay on top of details.

2. **Raise your hand.** Whether it is in your job, your church, or an organization that needs volunteers, raise your hand. Take on a job that is not being done or that is not being done well. Ask the overseers to allow you to handle a problem or to polish an area of weakness in your organization. Remember what I mentioned previously: lazy and inefficient people do not get promoted. However, those who take initiative and excel do. Lastly, when you commit to taking on a task, complete the task with excellence. You will be noticed and given more responsibility, just like Joseph was noticed.

3. **Clean up your own personal messes.** Recognize that messes are simply that—they are messes, and messes need to be cleaned up. Realize that they *should* be cleaned up because messes monopolize your much-needed mental capacity and daily bandwidth. Messes are comparable to a home remodel project; you don't know exactly what you are getting into until you tear into the walls.

   Thus, commit to having your personal paperwork messes cleaned out, organized, and completed within the next sixty days. For this to happen, you need to make a list of all those areas in your life that are secretly causing you stress. Clean them up and be done with them. Assign a project name to them and give yourself a deadline for completion. Once completed, you will immediately feel an enormous load lifted off your shoulders.

4. **Commit to learning a new technology.** New technology is the bane of my existence. It sometimes seems as if the number of new gadgets on the market doubles every six months. There is always some new device or

app that is being touted to "simplify" your life, and while sometimes that is true, many times it is not. A positive example of learning new technology happened to me during the COVID-19 shutdowns, when I committed to learning a new video conferencing platform—and I am so thankful I did! I, like so many others during this time, have relied on this technology to keep moving forward.

To learn new technology, commit to not being afraid of it. Instead, embrace it. Use the technology you need and discard the rest. Learn new technology but keep your life simple in doing so.

5. **Commit to staying organized daily.** There are so many things going on in everybody's world that can either be welcomed or unwelcomed distractions. *Inc.* magazine lists six easy steps to staying organized daily.[1]

1. **Set realistic goals and stay focused on them.** Your goals are the North Star that you'll follow day in and day out to achieve the success you desire.

2. **Get a calendar and maintain it, always.** Whether it's an old-fashioned desk calendar or the latest synced-across-ten-devices app-based wonder, the key is to use it religiously.

3. **Set your priorities at the start of each day.** Devote twenty minutes at the beginning of your business day to set your priorities. Make this time yours

---

[1]Peter Economy, "6 Keys to Getting Organized," Inc.com, December 18, 2013, accessed August 12, 2020, https://www.inc.com/peter-economy/6-keys-to-getting-organized.html.

and yours alone by forwarding your phone to voicemail, ignoring your email, and keeping your schedule clear.

4. **Prioritize your priorities.** Tackle your top priority first and your lowest priority last.

5. **Tie up loose ends at the end of each day.** Set aside at least twenty minutes at the end of your business day to tie up loose ends.

6. **Clean up your workspace.** It's hard to stay organized and on top of your most important tasks and priorities when your desk or your office is a mess. Take an hour or two every week to organize the paperwork that is no doubt taking over every inch of surface area.

I am going to take the liberty to add one more to this list:

7. **Learn to delegate.** We will discuss delegation in the next chapter.

Summary

These are seven easy steps to staying organized every day and taking these steps will boost your administration skill set either at work or at home. Learn from our biblical example Joseph, who was a master at administration. He invested in himself during his first thirteen years in Egypt. Investing in yourself will pay huge dividends down the road, both personally as well as professionally. These steps will help you excel in the gift of administration, but you must commit to taking steps to move forward. Every day, choose to hone your administrative skill set by learning something new.

CHAPTER 2
MOSES - A MAN OF DELEGATION

It was an early, mid-winter Sunday morning in 1987, and I was at church early to set up an information table for the prison ministry. I was attending a mega church in those days. Securing a spot for my insert in the Sunday bulletin was not easy, because space was always in high demand. An additional reason for my early arrival was that I needed everything to go smoothly; prison ministry was a new and intimidating ministry for many. Needless to say, I was showing some signs of stress that morning.

My stress was not baseless. Since starting in prison ministry in 1984, the recruitment process had been slow-going. Not many people were interested in going to prisons to preach to inmates. Those that did come forward were worth their weight in gold. I valued them and they were my heroes. They were individuals whom God had called out of their ordinary lives to be used by Him for higher purposes. However, because the pool of workers who came forward was so small, it isn't surprising many of these volunteers were also the "rascally" type. One such volunteer was Rico.

My relationship with Rico began when he came up and introduced himself to me after one of these Sunday services. I'll admit that my first visual impression of him was not good. This man sported long, greasy hair that was pulled back in a ponytail and he wore tinted sunglasses, a black felt hat that was tilted to one side, and thick gold chains around his neck. I remember thinking that he resembled a Latina mafia leader from the 1950s! Having come from the conservative world of finance as a stockbroker, Rico's demeanor immediately set my red flags flying.

Rico then asked me if I was "the prison guy" here at the church. My heart immediately sank because I knew what he would say next: "I want to get involved in prison ministry." And sure enough, he did. This perturbed me because only two years prior, the Lord had slapped me up the side of the head when He started sending laborers to the ministry whom I had prejudged and rejected simply because of the way they looked. I'd rejected them as potential volunteers because of my preconceived idea about what I thought a volunteer should look like. I was a conservative stockbroker thinking our volunteer base should look professional. How wrong I was!

Rico, however, was a different story than the rest. He truly *was* weird! In fact, he was so different from other volunteers (even the strange ones) that he was in a league of his own weirdness. His dress was gaudy, and his mannerisms were goofy. He also never called me by my first name, always addressing me as *Papa*. After spending some time with him, I wondered if I could even stand taking this man into the jails and prisons with me. However, not wanting another "head slap" from the Lord, I took a leap of faith and began the process of obtaining Rico's clearance for the King County Jail.

What I learned in the end was that Rico was faithful and always on time. He always conducted himself as a man of God when tasked with various assignments, and he always showed maturity and eloquence when handling Scripture.

It was on another Sunday morning when I was about to conduct my first pulpit interview at our church when Rico gave me some advice that changed my entire outlook on ministry.

"Papa, what's wrong?" Rico asked me that day.

"Nothing."

"Don't tell me nothing, you are bouncing around like a Spanish jump'n bean."

"Rico, I'm stressed. I'm supposed to be in front of the congregation today, but nothing is going right. The table in the lobby was not set up like it should be, my materials aren't here yet, and service starts in twenty minutes."

"Why are you doing this to yourself? It is going to be fine and you are going to do great."

"But nothing is ready out here in the lobby."

"You are being a Martha. Stop it! You are worrying over things you ought not worry about. You need to do as Moses did."

"What's that, Rico?

"The Moses approach, Papa, the Moses approach."

After the service, Rico hung around to give me a highly intense lesson on Moses' approach to delegation. I listened, I heard, I ruminated, and what he shared that day still resonates with me now. I learned that by taking baby steps, I could let go of responsibilities and empower others to take on more, thus lightening my work load and minimizing my stress.

The passage Rico pulled from was Exodus 18:14, when Jethro chides his son-in-law Moses for being what we would call today a "workaholic" or "a control freak."

> When his father-in-law saw all that Moses was doing for the people, he said, "What is this you are doing for the people? Why do you alone sit as

judge, while all these people stand around you from morning till evening?" (vs. 14).

Moses' father-in-law replied, "What you are doing is not good. You and these people who come to you will only wear yourselves out. The work is too heavy for you; you cannot handle it alone. Listen now to me and I will give you some advice, and may God be with you. You must be the people's representative before God and bring their disputes to him. Teach them his decrees and instructions and show them the way they are to live and how they are to behave (vs. 17-20).

But select capable men from all the people—men who fear God, trustworthy men who hate dishonest gain—and appoint them as officials over thousands, hundreds, fifties, and tens. Have them serve as judges for the people at all times but have them bring every difficult case to you; the simple cases they can decide themselves. That will make your load lighter because they will share it with you. If you do this and God so commands, you will be able to stand the strain, and all these people will go home satisfied" (vs. 21-23).

The Spirit of the Lord impressed upon Moses the importance of delegating responsibility early in his ministry. As leaders, we need to clone ourselves, so to speak, by searching for competent God-fearing men and women who hate dishonest gain and who are willing to serve as overseers of your company, church, or organization. Once you find those qualified new leaders, you will then need to pour your life into theirs, discipling them in the ministry that they will oversee.

If we examine these verses more closely, we will discover some wise principles throughout them as well. (Please note when we say "men," we are using the generic term which applies to both men and women leaders.)

1. **Select capable men.** This advice is of primary importance. As a ministry, we need to find people suited to carry the workload. Not everyone is "capable" in this area of leadership. We first identify people who are either spiritually gifted in leadership or who are "diamonds in the rough"—people who have the potential to become a leader but need some training to develop their gifts.

2. **Men who fear God.** This category would include people who genuinely have an intimate walk with the Lord and who understand that a biblical love of God should be balanced with a true fear of the Lord!

3. **Trustworthy men who hate dishonest gain.** The people we want on the leadership team are God-fearing people who understand what it means to be trustworthy, even in small matters. It is important that they have humble hearts and no other agenda than to win souls for Christ. They must also want to build up the kingdom of God here on earth through discipleship.

In a nutshell, Moses learned that effective leaders manage people by multiplying and delegating the workload to others. Thus, delegation is actually a solid biblical management principle.

It is humbling for me that this lesson on proper biblical delegation came not from the pulpit, but from an unlikely source—my friend Rico. This was a man who had lived on the dark side of life for many years of his pilgrimage; he was my long-haired, gold-chained friend, and a former inmate. And what he showed me shaped my ministry for decades and still does to this very day.

One last thing to note here is that while it was easy receiving this new teaching from Rico, implementing and executing the new concepts was not. I knew in my heart of hearts that if the ministry was ever to grow beyond me, I would need to wrap my hands around this teaching, shed my control-freak nature, and allow others to help me in carrying the load.

The "hot potato approach" to expanding the ministry

As the ministry began growing, so was my need for delegation (or what I called "Rico's teaching on the Moses approach to ministry")! I developed systems in my off hours so that someone could take my place, and then I trained others on how I wanted the administration to flow. I would start by overseeing everything, and then I would slowly (in some cases quickly) wean myself away from them—something that isn't always easy for me to do.

I will never forget the first time one of my key leaders wanted to change a process in the administrative area which I had created. She called me to explain that while the current process in place was sound and thoughtful, she felt if we tweaked one area it would make things run even smoother. In my mind, however, my pride set in. I thought to myself, "How dare she change *my* process?" The Holy Spirit took me to task and by the end of the phone call, I told her I trusted her. And since the framework of the system was solid, she could tweak it to make it even better. She had my permission to go for it—and she did, with great gusto! To this day, we still use some of her suggestions in our day-to-day operation of the ministry.

The point here is that if you are wired for growth and wired for leadership, you need to let go. Understanding the Moses approach to delegation is imperative to growing any type of God-ordained ministry.

I also call this the "hot potato approach of letting go." Once the system for administration has been designed, the people have been trained, the system has been tested, and the bugs have been worked through, you need to move out of the way and let your people thrive.

Letting them thrive, however, does not mean you should avoid evaluating them. I believe we, as administrators, are constantly in need of evaluating systems and practices. My good friend and fellow board member Don Szolomayer often says, "Inspect what you expect." I keep this in mind whenever I bring someone new on board. It does not matter if he is a new volunteer or a new employee, I always begin by explaining the current system. Then I say, "This is how I want this to run. No changes for six months. After six months, once you are comfortable with the systems and procedures, if you want to make changes then do so and record your changes in the training manual for those who come behind you." This system has worked very well for the ministry.

Over the years, I've also realized that while ministries need to have volunteers, they will also eventually need paid staff members, too. In our early years, we had volunteers doing the back-office operations of the ministry. We eventually learned that the number of jobs we needed them to do outgrew the amount of volunteer time per week they could invest in those responsibilities. When that happens to you as an administrator, you will find yourself at a crossroad. Should you stay where you are and plateau, or should you go to the next level? The next level is transforming the volunteer positions into part-time or full-time paid staff positions.

What can we learn from the life of Moses?

Moses lived one hundred and twenty years—three sets of forty years each. In the first forty years, Moses lived as a member of the royal family in Pharaoh's household. He was schooled in all aspects of royal living. In the second forty years of his life, he lived in the land of Midian as a shepherd. What a contrast. Finally, in the last forty years, he led a nation of over a million people out of Egypt. What can we learn from the life of Moses? Let me list six Leadership Life Principles below.

Leadership Life Principle #1: Learn to listen to God. Moses listened to God. Moses met God at the burning bush. Although he had great reservations about what God had called him to do, he ultimately went and fulfilled God's purposes for his life. Although he argued with God five different times, he finally went. As leaders, we need to listen to God. We need to listen to Him without the clutter of hidden agendas screaming to the inner man.

Leadership Life Principle #2: Commit to being teachable. Moses was extremely teachable. His father-in-law observed a potential problem and approached him about it. Moses listened to Jethro and implemented his suggestions. Although Moses could have ignored Jethro's sound advice (perhaps choosing not to listen to his father-in-law simply because he *was* his father-in-law), Moses didn't—such a rejection of sound advice would have been rooted in pride.

Leadership Life Principle #3: Learn to lead many. Moses led over a million people through the desert for forty years. Although he was never allowed to enter the Promised Land, Moses led over a million people as they wandered in the desert. This was no easy task. Even the Lord called the people a "stiff-necked" people.

Leadership Life Principle #4: Learn to be humble at all times. Moses was a humble person, and God often uses humble people to carry out His agenda. To illustrate, Moses was a shepherd when God spoke to him from a burning bush. He was tending the family flock and had no aspirations of going back to Egypt to live in the royal household. Instead, he had chosen to spend the last forty years in the land of Midian. One may assume that he was content with this new way of life since this life change was a personal decision of his, though the Bible is silent on this matter. All we know is that he was married and raised a family of his own during those years.

Leadership Life Principle #5: Allow God to fight your battles for you. Moses allowed God to fight his battles for him. Likewise, if we let Him, God will fight the battles for His children. The Bible is replete with stories of God doing supernatural works on behalf of His children. Isaiah 58 is the "Hall of Fame" chapter for fasting—it gives us twelve promises the Bible says could occur if we fast properly. Verse 8 contains the fourth of the twelve promises: "The righteousness will go before you, and the glory of the LORD will be your *rear guard*" (emphasis added). Isn't that what we all desire, to have the Lord watching over us, being our rear guard, fighting on our behalf against the enemy?

Leadership Life Principle #6: Implement the art of delegating. Moses learned to delegate. To lead a million people through the desert for forty years, Moses surely had to learn leadership principles—one of which must have been the principle of delegation.

Why don't people delegate more?

There are several reasons people don't delegate. Several of these reasons are rooted in sin issues—pride and fear. The other reasons vary. Your reason could simply be not having anyone to whom you can delegate. Or, it may be that you are the low man on the totem pole. Or, if you are in a hiring position maybe you haven't hired enough staff for your growing organization. The reasons are numerous and understanding them may be key to helping you delegate more. Below are seven reasons why people don't delegate:

1. **You are the biggest obstacle to delegating.** Let's face it. You're it! You are the number one reason you don't delegate. If you only knew what freedom proper delegation could provide to your daily schedule, you'd probably do it. It sounds counterintuitive, but this is the truth. You might even find that you'll be promoted if you delegate well, because delegation will enable you to accomplish more and be more productive. And once promoted, you may also receive a pay raise.

2. **You fear the job won't get done right.** Although this is a real concern of many, it is still rooted in the sin of fear. This is when you fear things which have not occurred. You are letting your mind run with the "what ifs." You are not allowing God to work through you or your subordinates. You fear you will be embarrassed

by shoddy work or that you will have to redo work that doesn't meet your perfectionist attitude.

3. **If you want a job done right, you must do it yourself.** This is an attitude that is firmly rooted in the sin of pride. You view yourself as the only one qualified to do the job. You hold yourself in a higher regard than anyone else for getting the work done.

4. **It will take you longer to explain it, than to do it yourself.** This too, is an attitude that is rooted in the sin of pride because it is based on the high opinion of your own skill set. You are essentially saying that no one else is as good or as quick as you are.

    I'll admit that I can personally relate to this attitude. Sometimes I indulge in an internal sigh before embarking down this road. I have come to realize that while it may take longer to explain a process to someone, doing so will demonstrate that you want to invest in your staff. Remember, as an administrator, you are in it for the long haul.

5. **Losing control.** This is the sin of fear. Let's face it, if this is your reason for not delegating, you are a control freak. You are working yourself into an early grave or into divorce court. Working with control freaks only frustrates people, and frustrated people tend to leave. Being a control freak usually leads to a high employee turnover rate. This, in turn, continuously resets the delegation "clock." If you are always hiring new staff, you will never have anyone you trust for delegation.

6. **Not getting the credit.** This too is rooted in pride. Why? Simply put, you want to be acknowledged as the

superstar. Give credit where credit is due. Share the credit. Keep the credit loosely. If you freely give credit, you too will be promoted. This will in turn encourage your team to work harder for you and for the team.

7. **Lack of trust.** You don't trust the person to whom you are delegating. This may or may not be a valid reason for not delegating. If someone has sabotaged you before, then of course, you need to be careful. On the other hand, if you honestly believe someone doesn't have the skill set, the capacity to learn, or the ability to make team deadlines, should that person even be on your team?

How can you overcome these obstacles?

To hone your skills as an excellent delegator, you need to be on point every day, determined to overcome any of the above obstacles. Evaluate yourself in your areas of weakness. Commit to the following seven potential solutions:

1. **Choose the right person for the right job!** Let's say you have a team of eight. By applying the bell-shaped curve that you learned in your college statistics class, you can assume that in a team of eight, two will be overachievers, four will be middle-of-the-road producers, and two will be bringing up the tail end. Your job is to constantly motivate your team to reach their next level of growth. Analyze your project and start divvying up the job assignments according to their abilities, so that they are assigned a task that is barely above their reach. Never let anyone get too comfortable within their assignments or job descriptions. To be fair to your team, you may need to invest in additional training

or office hardware to bring their skill set to the next level, and to enable them to complete the tasks that you've assigned them.

2. **Give clear instructions.** I can't tell you how many times I thought I was as clear as a bell in my instructions, only to receive work back that looked totally different than what I had envisioned. One way to prevent this from happening is to have your staff repeat back to you what you explained to them. Any discrepancy between what you said and what your staff heard needs to be immediately clarified.

3. **Allow room for creativity.** As mentioned above, there have been times when I thought I had clearly spelled out my instructions. Furthermore, there were times when I would even ask staff to repeat my instructions back to me and ask them if they had any questions. I still would receive something back totally different than what I had imagined. I have since changed my tactics.

    Tell your staff what your expectations are and what you want to see. Giving people freedom for their own creativity allow them the liberty to inject their own ideas into the project. Once I have shared with them my expectations, I give staff editorial freedom to try their own ideas in addition to mine. I then tell them I want to see both samples side by side, my original idea and their own take on it. More times than not, their ideas are better than mine.

4. **Have other people give the instructions.** Sometimes there are people who can do a great job but who don't communicate well with you. In cases like this, I

use a middleman. I give the middleman—usually someone else in a position of leadership in the office—my specific instructions on what I want, tell him or her to assign the task to the other person, and then to oversee the project. The job always comes back spot on. Had I given the instructions directly to the person in question, the end result would have come back totally wrong.

5. **Get your fear under control.** One of the main tools the enemy uses to render believers ineffective for the cause of Christ is fear. Fear neutralizes everything. In the Bible, there are three hundred and sixty-five references to "fear not!" Fear stops us from wanting to learn how to delegate. We discussed fear being an obstacle to proper delegation. One method of overcoming fear is to mitigate any potential for not meeting deadlines in the projects you assign.

One way you can overcome feeling stressed over time deadlines is to give yourself and your team a good deal of lead time. I use the 2-1-2-1 model. Every Monday I scan my calendar for tasks or projects on the horizon that are two months out, one month out, two weeks out, and one week out. If you incorporate this model (or a similar model to meet your own preferences) into your management routine, you can alleviate much of the stress over surprise impending deadlines.

6. **Give plenty of kudos.** One of the main reasons people leave an organization is that they do not feel appreciated. Studies show that people are not always motivated by high salaries or titles, but more so because they feel appreciated and part of a larger team. Thus, it

goes without saying that leaders should direct compliments to their team members when they've done a good job. These compliments can come verbally, in written form, or in special monetary rewards, such as gift cards or time off. You can also decide if you want to compliment them publicly or privately.

Also, did you know that you can buy gift cards electronically through Amazon and send them directly to a person's email address? There are as many different types of gift cards online as there are in the grocery stores' end-cap gift card displays. You can do this right from your computer. So cool! What a time saver and one that will pay huge dividends later on.

"Giving kudos" is an area I need to work on myself. This is not because I am stingy with my compliments, but because I can be slightly introverted. It takes work for introverts to come out of their shells, but it is work worth doing.

7. **Understand in the beginning it may take longer than if you did it yourself.** This is one of the several reasons I listed as why people don't do more delegating. The only way you can mitigate this is to be more proactive and proficient in planning your timeline. If you will incorporate the 2-1-2-1 planning model as explained above, you can put this issue to bed.

Summary

Learning to delegate for a new leader can be frightening, especially if you have deadlines looming, or if your boss is crawling down your neck. However, delegation is one of the most essential tools you should put into your leadership tool belt. Learn to delegate successfully and you will leverage your time and your day. And for the more mature leaders, you may already be a master at delegating, but continue to look at new ways of leveraging your time by offloading some of your daily tasks. Use the tools in the appendix to self-determine where you could increase your abilities.

CHAPTER 3

NEHEMIAH - A MAN OF GREAT VISION

If the book of Nehemiah were an article of clothing, it would be one of those enduring pieces that never goes out of style. Nehemiah is an all-time classic book of the Bible, a timeless book about leadership. I have read Nehemiah through many times and will continue to do so in the future. Yet, despite my excitement over using it as the foundation of this section, I still struggled to create a tagline for this chapter. There were many different descriptions I could have assigned to Nehemiah, but I ended up choosing *A Man of Great Vision*. This is an action-packed book with both intrigue and potential sabotage. But what can we learn from Nehemiah, a man of great vision, on this topic of leadership? I believe there are twelve life lessons that can be learned by examining the life of Nehemiah more closely.

Leadership Life Principle #1: People of vision are moved to action by some external input. Many great men and women of vision are motivated by an idea. This idea might be a solution to an organization's problem or even a world problem, an idea that addresses social injustices, a desire to build a "better mouse trap," or even an answer to a missionary calling. When we start reading the book of Nehemiah, we learn right away about his motive for action—it's the news of the disgraceful condition of his beloved city, Jerusalem. He learns that the wall of Jerusalem has been torn down. Before he plans to rebuild it, however, Nehemiah first sits down to mourn and weep over the crisis.

> Hanani, one of my brothers, came from Judah with some other men, and I questioned them about the Jewish remnant that had survived the exile, and also about Jerusalem.

> They said to me, "Those who survived the exile and are back in the province are in great trouble and disgrace. The wall of Jerusalem is broken down, and its gates have been burned with fire."

> When I heard these things, I sat down and wept. For some days I mourned and fasted and prayed before the God of heaven (Neh 1:2-4).

Leadership Life Principle #2: People of vision fast and pray before deciding on the course of action. I will tell you upfront when I am about to take a rabbit trail, and this is one of those times. As I researched Nehemiah from a leadership perspective, I came across no less than ten authors who espoused the great leadership principles in this book of Nehemiah. However, what I found quite interesting was that most of these leadership experts stated that great works of God always start with prayer. How could anyone disagree? I agree with that assessment wholeheartedly. Prayer should be an integral part of any job you are called to do.

To illustrate, notice again that when Nehemiah heard the tragic news of Jerusalem's disgrace, the Bible says that

Nehemiah "sat down and wept." This is a normal human emotion when one hears bad news; we feel shock, bewilderment, and then sorrow, which often arrives in the form of tears. Next, the Bible says Nehemiah "mourned and fasted and prayed" (Neh 1:4), in that order. What I find most interesting is that while most of these leadership experts acknowledge the importance of prayer, they tend to neglect addressing the power of fasting. However, I believe all great works of God should ultimately start with the power of fasting undergirded with a season of prayer.

I published a book in 2016 on biblical fasting called *Staving off Disaster- A Journey in Biblical Fasting.* I believe there is extraordinary power in biblical fasting when it is done right and with the right motives. The church is woefully undereducated in the power that fasting unleashes. To illustrate, I can post a picture of my wife and me on Facebook and receive over two hundred likes very quickly. When I share a post on fasting, however, I may get twenty-five likes. It's undeniable that Christians do not understand the act of fasting correctly or its implications! Our current situation in America with the COVID-19 crisis demonstrates this perfectly. How many Americans would fast with me over this national crisis? I dare say that very few would. It is also something to note that I get more comments on my fasting posts from my brothers and sisters in other countries than I do from my fellow Americans.

Unsurprisingly, the great task of rebuilding the wall that Nehemiah undertook started with fasting and prayer. The rebuilding of the wall was attacked six different times, escalating in severity each time. In fifty-two days the wall was finally completed. The naysayers of the time said it couldn't be done, but Nehemiah understood the strength of fasting before starting a work, and he coupled that with a season of prayer. Following this thought, I then reviewed this passage in ten other different translations of the Bible—all of which used the word *fasting*. Why, then, would other leadership experts not address the topic of fasting?

Leadership Life Principle #3: People of vision count the costs before starting any major project. Just as you would need to think ahead and budget before booking a vacation, leaders need to think ahead before starting major projects. It is also prudent that leaders seek God's favor in the task, just as Nehemiah prayed, "Give your servant success today by granting him favor in the presence of this man [the king]." In the last chapter we asked, "Is it ok to pray to the Lord for favor surrounding a task?" My answer is that of course it is! This is yet another example of a man of God asking the Almighty for His favor; and, doing so is one way of "counting the costs" before starting.

To illustrate, God's favor on Nehemiah came in the form of favor with King Artaxerxes. Nehemiah was King Artaxerxes's cupbearer. He would test the King's wine to make sure no one had poisoned it and spent the bulk of his day in the presence of the king. Although he didn't have much authority in court, Nehemiah did have influence. God's favor showed itself when one day, the king noticed that Nehemiah's face was downcast. This event became the opening Nehemiah needed to present his vision and need to the king.

Leadership Life Principle #4: People of vision understand they need to make presentations to those who can aid them in their quest such as donors, stakeholders, bosses, superiors, or politicians. Nehemiah had a great "elevator pitch" in verses 2:3-8. He knew what he was going to say.

If it pleases the king and if your servant has found favor in his sight, let him send me to the city in Judah where my fathers are buried so that I can rebuild it.

I also said to him, "if it pleases the king, may I have letters to the governors of Trans-Euphrates, so that they will provide me safe-conduct until I arrive in Judah? And may I have a letter to Asaph, keeper of the kings forest, so he will give me timber to make beams for the gates of the citadel by the temple and for the city wall and for the residence I will occupy?

I suspect Nehemiah had practiced his pitch several times before he made it. Do you think such a bold pitch would have come naturally to him otherwise? Absolutely not! Observe what Nehemiah says in the latter part of 2:2. He says, "I was very much afraid." This is my hero saying that he was very much afraid. He knew what could happen if the king was displeased with a request—that person could literally lose his or her head.

However, Nehemiah had *fasted* and prayed, and that is why he had the holy boldness to share his need with the king. And, not only was he bold enough to ask for a leave of absence from his very important job—a job on which the king's life depended—Nehemiah also did some fundraising for this project as well! Nehemiah knew that he needed not only safe passage to Jerusalem, but also materials to rebuild the wall. Thus, he asked for it. The favor he had asked God for in verses 7 and 8 was granted. God moved on the king's heart to give Nehemiah all the resources he requested.

Leadership Life Principle #5: People of vision assess the current situation surrounding a project. The Bible says Nehemiah arrived in Jerusalem and was there for three days. I suspect he didn't immediately assess the damage in the city for several reasons. First, after such a long trip he needed to rest before doing that. Second, he didn't want to call attention to himself. This is evident when the Bible says he had told no one why he was there. When the time was right, he decided to take a nocturnal trip to evaluate the damage.

Leadership Life Principle #6: People of vision recruit a team to assist in executing a project. Visionaries know they cannot complete the work solely by themselves, either because the work is physically too demanding for one person or that they don't possess all the skills needed to complete the task. When I think of some of the secular visionaries today, I think of people such as Elon Musk, Jeff Bezos, and Bill Gates. These are men who were wise enough to surround themselves with some of the best minds in technology, science, and marketing to carry out their missions.

When I think of Christian businessmen, I think of Truett Cathy of Chick-fil-A, Dave Thomas of Wendy's, Sam Walton of Walmart, David Green of Hobby Lobby, and Norm Miller of Interstate Batteries. These men built huge companies based on biblical principles. Still, they also had to recruit some of the top business minds from around the country to assist them in executing their visions.

When I think of great men of God in our generation, I think of the late Billy Graham, his son Franklin Graham, Ravi Zacharias, and Luis Palau. They, too, surrounded themselves with great minds. The entire third chapter of Nehemiah tells us how he chose his team and assigned them each a piece of the project. Visionary leaders recruit the finest team they can find. They also understand that if they pay them well, give them a supportive environment in which they can excel, and provide them with positive motivation, then the mission of the organization will succeed, likely well beyond their expectations. Visionary leaders understand they are not "lone rangers." Nehemiah knew this as well.

Leadership Life Principle #7: People of vision train and instruct their team. Nehemiah gave specific people specific responsibilities and tasks to complete. Some built the walls, others built the gates, and some built both. Although chapter three includes many names we cannot pronounce, it demonstrates that not just a few people were working on the gates and walls—it was most likely the entire town. And when situations became dangerous with the possibility of an attack, Nehemiah gave the workers even further direction.

> From that day on, half of my men did the work, while the other half were equipped with spears, shields, bows and armor. The officers posted themselves behind all the people of Judah who were building the wall. Those who carried materials did their work with one hand and held a weapon in the other, and each of the builders wore his sword at his side as he worked. But the man who sounded the trumpet stayed with me.
>
> Then I said to the nobles, the officials, and the rest of the people, "The work is extensive and spread out, and we are widely separated from each other along the wall. Wherever you hear the sound of the trumpet, join us there. Our God will fight for us!"

So, we continued the work with half the men holding spears, from the first light of dawn till the stars came out. At that time, I also said to the people, "Have every man and his helper stay inside Jerusalem at night, so they can serve us as guards by night and workmen by day." Neither I nor my brothers nor my men nor the guards with me took off our clothes; each had his weapon, even when he went for water (Neh 4:16-23).

When there is need, a visionary leader puts out the call, "All hands on deck." Likewise, Nehemiah gave his people explicit instructions arming them for either work or for battle.

Leadership Life Principle #8: People of vision fight the battles that arise during their ventures. When you are working for the kingdom, there will be battles. Sometimes those battles come from the outside and other times they come from within the camp. Those battles that come from within are the hardest because you feel you are being betrayed by one of your own. In this story, Nehemiah experienced six different battles he had to overcome.

- From ridicule- 4:1-6
- From collusion- 4:7-23
- From exaction- 5:1-13
- From a threat of bodily harm- 6:1-4
- From a smear campaign- 6:5-9
- From intimidation- 6:10-13

Nehemiah was a man driven to succeed. These six threats were distractions from the enemy and Nehemiah saw them for what they were. If allowed to run uncontrolled, distractions can derail entire projects. Visionaries see distractions as either something to sidestep or a chance to do some creative problem solving.

Leadership Life Principle #9: People of vision execute the vision God has given to them. At any time Nehemiah could have said, "This isn't worth it. I am heading back home where I can continue being the king's cupbearer, where the food is better, the clothes are better, and the environment is better"—but he didn't. He kept pressing on for the completion of the project. Like Nehemiah, the Apostle Paul could have also chosen to quit when he faced adversity, but he didn't. We will discuss Paul later in this book.

Leadership Life Principle #10: People of vision manage to keep the team motivated during the mission. I have often wondered how Nehemiah kept his team motivated despite the distractions surrounding their circumstances. He found a way to capitalize on the principle found in Nehemiah 4:6, and this is a verse I have used many times when I've worked with volunteers. In it, Nehemiah says, "So we rebuilt the wall till all of it reached half its height, for the *people worked with all of their heart*" (emphasis added).

So, how can you motivate a team to work with all their heart? You can begin by asking them for their help, expressing appreciation, showing them how their help maximizes the organization's goals, making sure they are trained and have the tools to do their job, allowing flexibility in their schedules, and by having fun with them. In certain circumstances, even a good meal can be a motivating factor. I like to say, "Feed them and they will stay."

It is wise to note also that motivation was not lacking in Jerusalem during the rebuilding of the wall. This task was both a matter of personal security and of national pride for the Jews. If that was the case, then, why had the Jews who had been living in Jerusalem all along didn't rebuild the wall before Nehemiah had arrived? The answer is simple—although they had the manpower to fix the wall, the Jews had been lacking one important factor—Nehemiah's vision. You will find in life there are many who are motivated or passionate about certain causes, but who are incapable of carrying them out because they lack the vision.

We see a similar situation to Nehemiah's in Esther, about whom was written, "And who knows but that you have come to royal position for such a time as this" (Est 4:14). This verse refers to the fact that Esther became a royal at just the right time—a time when the Jews needed her most. In Esther's time, they were being threatened by Haman, and though many probably wished to do something about this persecution, many Jews undoubtedly felt helpless in their situation. Esther was just the right person to come to their rescue. Similarly, Nehemiah was also called to help the Jews who were in need. And because Nehemiah had served as a trusted person in the king's court and had learned the skill of diplomacy that was needed to carry off such a task as rebuilding Jerusalem's wall, he was able to do the job well. He also had the backing of the king. Like Nehemiah, many visionaries—because of the position they hold within the organization or community—can help keep their team motivated.

Leadership Life Principle #11: People of vision complete the task at hand. Nehemiah didn't stop when faced with adversity, he pressed on towards the goal. Likewise, visionaries complete the task at hand. I am reminded of the great entrepreneur Henry Ford who told his engineers that he wanted a V-8 engine. They said it was impossible and that it couldn't be built. After several rounds of meetings, Henry Ford became frustrated with his engineering team. He threatened that if they could not develop a V-8 engine within six months, he would fire them all. Guess what? Henry Ford got his V-8 engine. Though he used threats to motivate his team, he nevertheless found a way to provoke them enough to complete the task.

Correspondingly, I was six years old when President John F. Kennedy announced on May 25, 1961—to a joint session of Congress—that he wanted to put a man on the moon within the decade. I remember there was an outcry of "Impossible!" I was fourteen years old when my parents and I watched, on our black and white TV, Neil Armstrong step onto the surface of the moon and say, "One small step for man, one giant leap for mankind." An impossible task was completed because they had a leader with a vision.

Leadership Life Principle #12: People of vision praise the Lord upon completion. Christian visionaries understand from where their talents and blessings come. They understand some of their plans are so far beyond themselves that if God doesn't have His hand in them, they are doomed to failure. They immediately give glory to God for the small victories as well as the large victories. They understand that all blessings come from the Lord, and all skills are bestowed upon us from Him.

Summary

Let's review the twelve traits of men and women who are visionaries. Which of these are your strongest areas? Which of these are your weakest? Please take the test in the appendix under Exhibit A and B to assist you in identifying where you are the strongest and where you might need some help.

- People of vision are moved to action by some external input.
- People of vision fast and pray before deciding on the course of action.
- People of vision count the costs before starting any major project.
- People of vision understand they need to make presentations to those who can aid them in their quest such as donors, stakeholders, bosses, superiors, or politicians.
- People of vision assess the current situation surrounding a project.
- People of vision recruit a team to assist in executing a project.
- People of vision train and instruct their team.
- People of vision fight the battles that arise during their ventures.
- People of vision execute the vision God has given to them.
- People of vision manage to keep the team motivated during the mission.
- People of vision complete the task at hand.
- People of vision praise the Lord upon completion.

CHAPTER 4
DANIEL - A MAN ABOVE REPROACH

Most of us have never experienced a marauding army sweep through our country, take us captive, and carry us off to another country; but this is exactly what happened to Daniel. In 605 BC, the armies of Nebuchadnezzar attacked Jerusalem, seized Daniel and his three friends—Shadrach, Meshach, and Abednego—and carried them off to captivity in a foreign land. I personally can't even imagine being ripped away from my life in this country, separated from my family, and forced to learn a new culture with a new language; it's even more unfathomable when I think how young Daniel was at that time. Some say he could have been anywhere from ten to eighteen years old when he was taken into captivity.

But why were Daniel and his friends taken? The question as to why some were taken, and others were left behind is often debated. A common conclusion is that the conquering king chose only to take the "cream of the crop" of young people back to his country. Regardless of the reason he was taken, Daniel spent many formative years in captivity, serving as a government official under four different rulers—Nebuchadnezzar, Belshazzar, Darius, and Cyrus. It wasn't long before he was well-trained in the fine workings of the government.

At one point when Daniel served under King Darius, the king appointed "120 satraps to rule throughout the kingdom, with three administrators over them, one of whom was Daniel" (Dan 6:1-2). A satrap was a provincial governor with enormous power to impose laws and levy taxes. Satraps were trustworthy men to the king; they owned land and administered the property under the king's name. To understand the power Daniel now possessed, you need only look at the number of men who were appointed by Darius to govern these satraps—three! Daniel was one of the select *three* administrators. When Daniel was appointed to this position under King Darius, some say he was eighty years old with a government tenure of sixty years. That would mean that Daniel had been around the government workings for over six decades—and while this insinuates that he had plenty of time to learn the political system, it's conceivable that he also had time to make enemies in those years, too.

Verse 3 continues, "Now Daniel so distinguished himself among the administrators and the satraps by his exceptional qualities that the king planned to set him over the whole kingdom." This was a huge promotion for Daniel. However, it didn't take long before human nature reared its ugly head. His promotion angered certain individuals who thought they should have been promoted instead. Note that this type of mentality plays out across the corporate world daily.

Unsurprisingly, it didn't take long for the character assassination to begin. The administrators and satraps tried to find any area of Daniel's work life where he could be brought up on charges before the king. Though the Bible is silent on how many of the government officials participated in this conspiracy, it is obvious many were desperate to find some area of corruption in Daniel's work life. Unfortunately for these misanthropes, their efforts to bring him down were futile. Daniel 6:4 states that they "tried to find grounds for charges against Daniel in his conduct of government affairs, but they were unable to do so. They could find no corruption in him because he was trustworthy and neither corrupt nor negligent." Daniel had achieved the gold standard of ethical work behavior. This standard is even better synopsized in Colossians 3:23 which says, "Whatever you do, work at it with all of your heart, as working for the Lord, not for men."

It's interesting to note that often when corrupt people can't find a way to tear down their target's professional life, they often look at the target's personal life next. Has this ever happened to you? Has anyone ever brought an allegation or objection against you because of your personal beliefs, just for the purpose of getting you fired? How did you respond? How did others respond? In Daniel's story, when the mutineers could find nothing professionally wrong with Daniel, they also began looking at his personal life. They went so far as to convince King Darius to sign a decree that would be impossible to repeal, according to their federal laws. The decree declared that "anyone who prays to any god or man during the next thirty days, except to you, O king, shall be thrown into the lions' den." Thus, Daniel had a decision to make. He continued to pray to his God.

> Three times a day he got down on his knees and prayed, giving thanks to his God, just as he had done before (Dan 6:10).

You know the rest of the story. King Darius, under his own law which he could not repeal, was forced to throw Daniel into the lions' den. But God was faithful and closed the mouths of the lions. After Daniel emerged unharmed, King Darius had the administrators and the satraps who had engineered the whole plot—along with their wives and children—thrown into the den of lions.

What can we learn from the life of Daniel?

The internet is awash in leadership principles found in Daniel's story. These principles range from understanding commitment, to standing firm in one's belief, to holding fast to the power of prayer. While all of these are admirable traits, I believe—from a leadership standpoint—there are five other critical life principles that are found in Daniel chapter 6.

Leadership Life Principle #1: Live your life according to God's standards. This is a key principle. God created us. He also gave us the owner's manual for life, the Bible, which contains every conceivable life occurrence that we could ever imagine or need to overcome. There is nothing we can experience in this life that the Bible does not address. I believe the Bible is the source for every marriage counselor or mental health professional's ability to comfort their patients. The Bible addresses everything.

Throughout the year, many stories cross my desk—stories of the carnage resulting from poor decision making. It's difficult not to shake my head and think to myself, "If people had only abided in God's Word, they could have eliminated ninety percent of trials and tribulations they are experiencing." Sometimes these trials are unavoidable. These are the tornados of life which swoop down from the sky unannounced and wreak instant havoc on our personal lives. The COVID-19 crisis is one such trial that, at the time of this writing, is affecting the whole world in some way. Ninety percent of the trials in life are instigated by our own poor decisions, by our lusts, by our greed, by our pride. John attests to this when he writes in 1 John 2:15-17.

> Do not love the world or anything in the world. If anyone loves the world, the love of the Father is not in him. For everything in the world—the cravings of sinful man, the lusts of his eyes and the boasting of what he has and does—comes not from the Father but from the world. The world and its desires pass away, but the man who does the will of God lives forever.

King Solomon also speaks of this in Ecclesiastes 12:13. He says, "Fear God and keep his commandments, for this is the *whole duty* of man" (emphasis added). This sums it up. This is the end goal. This is our duty in life.

Leadership Life Principle #2: Live your life above reproach. Daniel lived his life above reproach. Daniel 6:4 says his accusers could not find any corruption in him because he had three traits. First, he was trustworthy. Second, he was not corrupt. Third, he was not negligent. Daniel 6 covers the topic of being above reproach in every aspect of your life—in your work life, personal life, and thought life. But what does being above reproach really mean?

Being above reproach means living your life in such a manner that if anyone accused you of any impropriety, corruption, or malfeasant, no accusations would stick because there would be no evidence of it. There would be nothing that any court could use against you to detain you, place you under arrest, or put you in jail. It means that if you were accused of anything, you would be acquitted because there would be no factual evidence to support any claims of wrongdoing against you. Daniel's accusers looked at his service as a governmental official to find anything that could discredit his leadership, thus disqualifying him from his promotion. In the end, they could find nothing because he had been living above reproach.

You might be wondering if being above reproach means living a perfect life. Are we even capable of being perfect people? The answer is incontestably "no." There is only one perfect person and that is Jesus Christ. Living above reproach doesn't mean you can't make honest mistakes. Rather, if refers to the behavioral issues that could cause you to have a black eye to your inner circle of family, friends, and associates.

I was given two pieces of advice when I started in the ministry back in 1989. They have stuck with me ever since. One friend advised that if I were to lead a ministry, then I needed to make sure I do nothing that could disqualify me from ministry. He said if I were to succeed in ministry without any scandals or divisions, then I should live with one hundred percent transparency, no secrets. I privately gulped when he told me this—it was such a tall order! My other friend advised me to live my life is such a manner that nothing would ever hit the front page of my hometown newspaper that would embarrass my mother. This second piece of advice was interesting and one that I didn't see coming. However, it did stick with me. As a leader, if your actions could potentially be negative front page news either in print or electronic media, you definitely should stop what you are doing.

Now the overseer must be *above reproach* (1 Tim 3:2, emphasis added).

Titus also discusses this issue, but instead uses the word *blameless* in Titus 1:7. He says, "Since an overseer is entrusted with God's work, he must be blameless." Living your life above reproach will give you incredible internal peace that will enable you to make better use of your time, whether that is with your family or the ministry. Problems and worldly entanglements are always counterproductive and only take up mental bandwidth. Purpose today to take proactive steps in ridding yourself of any lingering problems or entanglements.

Leadership Life Principle #3: When you work, work above reproach. We are all living under the original curse. God spoke to Adam after the episode of eating the forbidden fruit and basically said, "Cursed is the ground because of you. You will spend your days taking care of the ground in grueling labor to produce a living for yourself and your family." That is our destiny in life, so therefore we should determine to enjoy the work we are given, even when it is hard work. In Ecclesiastes, Solomon makes some brazen statements about such work.

> That everyone may eat and drink, and find *satisfaction in all his toil* — this is a *gift of God* (Eccl 3:13, emphasis added).

> So, I saw that there is nothing better for a man than to enjoy his work, because that is his lot (Eccl 3:22).

> Whatever your hand finds to do, do it with all your might (Eccl 9:10).

Finding enjoyment in your life calling is certainly a gift from God, yet many Christians today hate what they do. They often claim they are not being fulfilled in their jobs. However, Colossians 3:23 says, "Whatever you do, work at it with all you heart, as working for the Lord, not for men." What a powerful statement! If we could only grasp that concept allowing it to course through our veins, Christians would be happier and more fulfilled in their life calling.

For six decades, Daniel worked as a government official under four different kings. It would be well within human nature to have messed up at some point since we all make mistakes. Still, his accusers found nothing with which to indict him. Nothing! That speaks volumes of his character. I suspect that is why the king reacted the way he did when Daniel's accusers reminded the king that his edict could not be changed. "He [the king] was determined to rescue Daniel and made every effort until sundown to save him" (Daniel 6:14). It further states, "Then the king returned to his palace and spent the night without eating and without any entertainment being brought to him. And he could not sleep. At the first light of dawn, the king got up and hurried to the lions' den" (Dan 6:18-19). Notice that those kinds of actions were not the actions of someone who was indifferent to Daniel. Rather, it seems that King Darius truly did care for Daniel as one of his trusted advisors.

Leadership Life Principle #4: When you make a mistake, admit to it quickly. If you cannot quickly, reasonably, and easily correct a mistake made in your job, then go immediately to your superior and explain what happened. Doing this will help prevent the issue from escalating even further. I discuss this also in part one of this series, when I describe my typical reaction to an employee who comes to me admitting he's made a mistake. I try to remind myself that most mistakes are not catastrophic.

Some mistakes can be pretty bad. In the early eighties when I was a stockbroker, I once put the wrong stock symbol on the order ticket for a client. This happened back when we didn't have the internet to place orders, and instead used three-part carbon forms. This meant that if you accidentally inverted one letter of the stock symbol, the outcome could be cataclysmic. Whenever one of the brokers did this, it was especially sobering since the brokerage firm had hammered this point hard in our training to make sure we never made those mistakes. And of course, these mistakes were also painful since we would have to personally pay back the firm if our mistake resulted in a loss to the client.

It wasn't till the end of the day, after the market had closed, that I realized my mistake. I felt like I was going to vomit. If I had caught the error before the market had closed, I could have corrected it much sooner and minimized the loss. Unfortunately, I had to wait until the next morning to correct the mistake. It was the longest night I had ever experienced. I raced to the office at the crack of dawn to be prepared to enter new orders. By the time the market opened, both the stock I'd wrongly bought and the stock I should have bought moved against me, resulting in a whopping $5,000 loss to the client. This was a significant amount of money—especially in those days. I immediately popped up from my chair and went directly to my branch manager's office. I must have turned three shades of ashen gray because he immediately said to me, "Von Tobel, what did you just do?" I explained the situation. He immediately called New York and tried—to no avail—to get someone with authority to undo the trades. But it was too late. They wouldn't budge. He finally said, "This is what I am going to do. Because this is your first loss like this, I will split the loss with you 50/50." In essence, my boss was saying the branch, out of their reserves, would pay fifty percent of the losses and I would pay the other fifty percent of the losses out of future earnings. I was elated. Though it still was a costly learning experience, it was one which I never repeated.

When you make a mistake that you can't fix, be quick in owning it. If you try to hide it, or fix it yourself, you will dig an even bigger hole. Problems like that never go away, they just become bigger.

Leadership Life Principle #5: Do not throw in your hat with evil doers. In the early nineties as the ministry was taking root, Rhonda and I were approached by a nice Christian couple from our church with whom we had become friends. They unexpectedly asked us if we would join them in making a complaint to the senior leadership of our church about two of the pastors on staff. As I listened to their arguments against the pastors, I felt myself taking their side. I soon became enraged at the arrogance of the pastors. Looking back, I can see now that this couple had been calculative in coming to us for help; they knew because Rhonda worked on staff at the church and I led a sanctioned ministry, we would provide them with the credibility they needed to make their case against the pastors.

Over the ensuing weeks, Rhonda and I had discussed the situation several times. And though we enjoyed the company of that couple, neither of us felt comfortable in joining forces with them. We eventually told our new friends that we could not be a part of their endeavor. Almost instantly, our friendship ceased.

The Holy Spirit instantly took me to Numbers 16—Korah's rebellion. This is the biblical account of one man, Korah, who collected two hundred and fifty well-known community leaders to oppose Moses and Aaron (Num 16:1-3). In the final confrontation, Moses instructed the nation to move away from the tents of Korah, Dathan, Abiram and the other two hundred and fifty leaders. We read in verse 31 the outcome of this rebellion:

> As soon as he finished saying all this, the ground under them split apart and the earth opened its mouth and swallowed them, with their households and all Korah's men and all their possessions. They went down alive into the grave, with everything they owned; the earth closed over them, and they perished and were gone from the community.

The outcome for Korah and his rebels was much the same as those who conspired against Daniel. Daniel 6:24 reads, "At the king's command, the men who had falsely accused Daniel were brought in and thrown into the lions' den, along with their wives and children. And before they reached the floor of the den, the lions overpowered them and crushed all their bones." Both stories are dramatic demonstrations of how God feels about people who come against godly leaders. Take note that not only did the leaders of these rebellions lose their own lives, but their entire households lost their lives as well, both wives and children.

Even David understood this concept. Twice David had the opportunity to kill Saul, who had been attempting to assassinate David. David's response when he had an opportunity to kill Saul is a lesson for us thousands of years later. We read in 1 Samuel 24:6, "The LORD forbid that I should do such a thing to my master, the LORD's anointed, or lift my hand against him, for he is the anointed of the LORD." Once again in 1 Samuel 26:9-11,

> Don't destroy him! Who can lay a hand on the LORD's anointed and be guiltless? As surely as the LORD lives, he said, the LORD himself will strike him; either his time will come and he will die, or he will go into battle and perish. But the LORD forbid that I should lay a hand on the LORD's anointed.

Summary

The outcome of our story above with the couple who had befriended us was this: there were other extenuating circumstances (as there always are), but the couple was discredited, left the church, and we never saw them again. Had we allowed ourselves to become entangled in their web, we too may have been discredited.

Stay away from church politics and office politics. Don't join forces with people who have evil intent in their hearts to come up against godly leaders. Be above reproach as you move forward.

CHAPTER 5

SHADRACH, MESHACH, AND ABEDNEGO - MEN SECURE IN THEIR CONVICTIONS

The story of Shadrach, Meshach and Abednego in the fiery furnace is one of my all-time favorite stories of the Bible. When these three boys were taken into captivity, some estimate their ages to have been anywhere from eleven to thirteen years, and when we hear about them again, time has passed and they have grown into young men.

Their story began in Daniel 3:1, when King Nebuchadnezzar built a statue of himself that was ninety feet tall and nine feet wide. He summoned his royal officials to the dedication of the statue at which time he mandated that all people were to fall down and worship the statue of gold whenever they heard the sound of music. It was not long after his decree, his servants informed King Nebuchadnezzar that the three young men were not falling to their knees to worship his image. This news enraged the king, who immediately demanded the three young men's presence. He gave them one last chance to do as he instructed, or they would be cast into the furnace. The three young men, standing before the king who controlled their fate, responded to his threat in a most surprising way.

> O Nebuchadnezzar, we do not need to defend our-
> selves before you in this matter. If we are thrown
> into the blazing furnace, the God we serve can save
> us from it, and he will rescue us from your hand,
> O king. But even if he does not, we want you to
> know, O king, that we will not serve your gods or
> worship the image of gold you have set up. (Dan
> 3:16-18).

Look at the conviction of these guys! They didn't feel any
need to defend themselves (Dan 3:16). They were con-
vinced that God had the power to rescue them, regardless
of the king's decision (Dan 3:17). They expressed their
conviction by being ready to die for it, meaning that they
knew that their deaths were a definite outcome of this
event (Dan 3:18).

Unsurprisingly, their answer further enraged the king.
He instructed his soldiers to heat the furnace seven times
hotter than usual—a command that even resulted in the
deaths of the soldiers who escorted these three young men
to the opening of the furnace. Thus, the three young men
were cast into the furnace, and through an unfathomable
miracle, they did not burn alive. The king witnessed this
miracle, even noticing that a fourth person was walking
around with the three young men in the furnace.

Perplexed, the king finally brought them out unscathed.
Not one hair on their heads had been seared; they didn't
even smell of smoke! Listen to what King Nebuchadnezzar
declared after witnessing the miracle of the three emerging
from the fiery furnace unharmed:

> Praise be to the God of Shadrach, Meshach, and
> Abednego, who has sent his angel and rescued his
> servants! They trusted in him and defied the king's
> command and were willing to give up their lives

rather than serve or worship any god except their own God (Dan 3: 28).

I want to meet these three incredibly courageous young men someday in Heaven. From where did their internal strength come? These were three young men who had their entire adult lives ahead of them, yet they were willing to lay their lives down for the sake of their God. I love how the Bible quotes them in verse 16 as saying, "We do not need to defend ourselves before you in this matter." Some might call this an arrogant and unwise remark to have made to a powerful, narcissistic king. If so, why did they respond to the king in this manner—especially since their past dealings with government officials were known to be more tactful?

The answer is this: Their response was wrapped in spiritual conviction. But where did this conviction come from, and how does one attain this level of conviction? We are going to attempt to answer these two questions.

From where does conviction come?

Daniel 1:4 describes the attributes of these young men: "Without any physical defect, handsome, showing aptitude for every kind of learning, well informed, quick to understand, and qualified to serve in the king's palace." This one verse reveals five qualities that were exhibited by Daniel and his friends. It's interesting to note that out of the five qualities listed, two qualities had to do with their outward appearance and three had to do with their intellect. This meant that not only were these good-looking young men, but they were also very smart. Daniel 1:17 continues to say, "To these young men God gave knowledge and understanding of all kinds of literature and learning," and Daniel, in addition to all of the above intellectual qualities, "could understand visions and dreams of all kinds." So where does conviction come from? I list four possibilities below.

1. **Their family upbringing.** These were not ordinary young men. They were the "Brainiacs" of their world, having high IQs, and being extremely high functioning young men. Today, many young people with these qualities are often proud, arrogant, and self-absorbed. However, this was not the case for these young men in the book of Daniel. They were well-trained by their parents and communities before they were taken from their homeland. They consciously chose not to allow a new culture to shape them. Although they assimilated into their new society easily, they did not allow the new culture to sway them from the things of God.

   Of course, having a great upbringing in a Christian home does not necessarily guarantee that good kids stay the course and do not go astray. Franklin Graham, Billy Graham's son, is a prime example of that rebellion found in kids who have been raised in a good Christian home. In his book, *Rebel and the Cause*, Mr. Graham shares in depth about his early rebellious years.[2] On the flipside, even if you were born to parents who lacked good parental skills, that does not guarantee that you will be disqualified as a godly leader later in life. When you are born again in Christ, you are a "new creation; the old is gone, and the new has come" (2 Cor 5:17).

2. **Their knowledge of God.** These young men were schooled in knowing the God that had designed the complexities of their bodies, as well as the Creator who

---

[2] Franklin Graham, *Rebel with a Cause* (Nashville, TN: Thomas Nelson, 1995).

made and sustains the universe. They had a full under-standing of God and were tutored in their Jewish her-itage. Having this foundation allowed them to stand up to the king's verbal abuse and his threats.

3. **Their faith in God.** Reading how they responded to the king helps me tremendously in building my faith. They make me strive to be more a man of conviction. These men told the king, "If we are thrown into the blazing furnace, the God we serve can save us from it, and he will rescue us from your hand, O king. But even if he does not, we want you to know, O king, that we will not serve your gods or worship the image of gold you have set up" (Dan 3:17). Why are we so astonished by this bold statement to the king?

    If our faith is strong, these verses should instead be part of our spiritual "life blood," giving us the power to stand firm in even the most severe trials. This faith statement is an example of their core values and their firm belief that God was more than able to deliver them from any trial. What trials are you walking through as a leader right now? Do you have faith that the Lord can deliver you from those trials? If He doesn't answer your prayers as you think they should be answered, where will you be in your faith walk? Will you become angry at God for being silent or for not answering your prayers? Will you turn your back on God? These three young men are examples for us to-day as we walk through turbulent times in our lives. Stand firm. Have faith in your Savior Jesus Christ.

4. **Their Devotion to God.** They had a devotion to their God that was unshakable. They were willing to go their deaths rather than compromise themselves by bowing

down to a ninety-foot statue. That's devotion! I am confident they were like any other young man at the time wanting families, wives, and kids. They undoubtedly aspired for better lives, but their devotion to God was bigger than the desires of their hearts. This is how we should be, standing firm and contending for the faith.

How does one maintain this level of conviction?

In my life, I need men around me to protect me from wandering from the faith or impaling myself on the world's lusts and schemes. I am blessed to have men like this who are very loyal to me. Some of them have even told me that if I ever screw up, tarnishing the name of Christ or the Christian faith, they would deal swiftly with me. They have also guaranteed me that it would not be pretty! As they protect me, it is my honor and privilege to do the same for them. This is a living example of my life in Proverbs 27:17 when it says, "As iron sharpens iron, so one man sharpens another."

Have you ever tried to use a dull knife to cut through something? It can be downright difficult and very frustrating. Practically speaking, that knife is worthless. Does a knife that has become dull stop being a knife? No, it is still a knife, just a less effective one. Conversely, a knife that has been sharpened becomes more effective for its designed purpose. As Christians, we were created to shine and reflect the image of our Creator, to be effective at ministering to a lost and dying world. Hebrews 4:12 says, "For the word of God is living and active. Sharper than any double-edged sword, it penetrates even to dividing soul and spirit, joints and marrow."

When a knife becomes dull, you have two options: you can throw the knife away, or you can sharpen it. The easiest way to sharpen a knife is to use a honing rod that comes with many cutlery sets. You take the dull knife and slide it across the honing rod. Through this repeated process on both sides of the blade, the heat and the friction caused by two materials passing over one another sharpens the knife. This is what Proverbs 27:17 means when it says that "one man sharpens another." One man is the knife needing to be sharpened and the other is the honing rod.

This is what I believe Shadrach, Meshach and Abednego had going for them. Before they ever faced the test of having to choose between compromising their beliefs or facing certain death, these men grew up as friends, sharpening one another. It is much easier to face struggles when you have people like these three young men surrounding you every day. Do you have those types of relationships in your life?

For the most part, women have an easier time making friends than men do. For most men, this does not come naturally. I have known several men who have never had another male friend in their lives. While this is sad, it can also be extremely dangerous. To illustrate, we can look at the many mass shooting perpetrators in America. Many of them fall in the same category—they are men who had no one in their lives, no male authority figure, no friends. It is statistically proven that many of these mass shooters were also loners in school as well as in their private lives. Those facts should cause you to stand up and take notice. As the days in this world become darker and darker, we need to surround ourselves with those who hold true to the biblical values near and dear to our hearts.

Gregory E. Von Tobel

What can we learn from the story of Shadrach, Meshach, and Abednego?

Leadership Life Principle #1: Understand that the trials of life are not necessarily an indication of God's withdrawal or His punishment. In America, we often pass judgement on those who are struggling with trials. We automatically believe if people are going through fire after fire, that something is wrong with their walk. We assume that perhaps they have done something that has caused the Almighty to cast them aside. We need only read 2 Corinthians 11:23-29 when Paul lists his many struggles in ministry to understand this thought is far from accurate. We can even look at the life of Job when his friends questioned him on what he did to anger God.

Following that train of thought, if Shadrach, Meshach and Abednego lived today, we might be wondering what they did to earn the judgment of God on their lives. What hidden sin were they all participating in to merit this judgement? Obviously, the Bible makes no reference to any sin in their lives, demonstrating how this cancerous thinking is simply not from God. This thinking comes from living in a prosperous society like America, where it is ingrained in us from the moment we start school that those who excel will be rewarded. In this story, however, we are reminded that these three young men were cast into a blazing furnace because of the will of God being worked in their lives. As my good friend Bob Jordan has repeatedly said, "God got the glory and Satan got a mouthful of dust." What are you going to do to stop passing judgment on people who are walking through the fiery furnaces of life?

Leadership Life Principle #2: Instead of pleading with God to extricate you from the fiery furnace of trials, discover Jesus in the fire. It is a normal thing when

68

we are living a hellish nightmare of a firestorm or walking through a desert that seemingly will never end, to cry out, "God, get me out of here! Make it stop!" I have prayed those prayers on certain occasions and in different seasons of my life. David, in Psalms, numerous times cried out to God.

> How long, O LORD, Will you forget me forever? How long will you hide your face from me? How long must I wrestle with my thoughts and every day have sorrow in my heart (Ps 13:1-2).

> To you I call, O LORD my Rock, do not turn a deaf ear to me. For if you remain silent, I will be like those who have gone down to the pit. Hear my cry for mercy as I call to you for help, as I lift my hands towards your Most Holy Place (Ps 28:1-2).

> Be pleased, O LORD, to save me; O LORD, come quickly to help me (Ps 40:13).

Scientists tell us there are over one hundred billion nerve cells in our bodies. The purpose of these nerves is to send impulses to the brain about potential problems such as pain, then to alert the body to do something to alleviate that pain. It is a natural response to feel pain and want it to stop immediately, whether it is physical or psychological.

In this example of the fiery furnace, Shadrach, Meshach, and Abednego met a fourth person in the fire. It was obvious that those who watched what happened recognized this person as a supernatural being. We can't be certain, as the Bible does not specify who the fourth person was, but many scholars believe this could have been a pre-incarnate Jesus.

The next time you are walking through the fiery furnace of life's trials, look for Jesus in the fire. When you look for Him, you will find Him, even during your darkest days. I suspect that as we enter the end days, our struggles will become more frequent and more pronounced. Purpose to surround yourself with competent, loyal friends whose iron will sharpen your iron.

Leadership Life Principle #3: We will never lead a dying world to Christ by blending in with the mainstream culture. This is evident in the lives of Shadrach, Meshach, and Abednego. These three young men did not blend into the culture of the day, even when they were asked to bow down to a statue made of gold. They knew this one act of disobedience could begin a pattern of sin and compromise in their lives. They knew they did not want that outcome. Instead, they chose to stand out. One of the takeaways of this biblical narrative is that even though standing out can get you into an abundance of trouble, we should never shrink back from the mandate of the Great Commission. No matter how tempting it is to simply give in and be like everyone else.

Many believers today try to blend into the culture. This is one of the problems I have had with a Christian cliché that was traveling the Christian circuit thirty years ago called *lifestyle evangelism*. This form of evangelism means living a life that your neighbors and coworkers would observe and want to be a part of. My issue with lifestyle evangelism is that it is passive, and sharing the Gospel should be active. People are dying and going to hell daily—now is certainly not the time to be passive about one's eternity. Yet, I have still seen lifestyle evangelism used by Christians as an excuse to be passive in their commitment to sharing the Good News of Jesus Christ. These dark days are not a time to hold back and it is certainly not a time to blend into the accepted culture of the day.

Leadership Life Principle #4: Understand that if God answered all our prayers the way we want, there would be no reason for faith. We serve a mighty God. His ways are not our ways. He is sovereign and we are not. If we had a God who answered our prayers the way we want all the time, we would not need to build our faith muscle. He would just be a "genie in a bottle" whom we could access whenever we are in trouble or want something. If He answered all our prayers one hundred percent of the time the way we thought our prayers should be answered, there would be absolutely no reason for us to have faith. The Bible is clear that without faith, it would be impossible to please God.

Leadership Life Principle #5: Realize that to be a leader who understands conviction, you need to get out on the limb and be counted. I have been so far out on the limb of trust during different stages of my life that I have become familiar with its surroundings. This is not necessarily a good thing because it can breed a cavalier spirit, and having a cavalier spirit is simply the sin of pride in a new set of clothes. This is a place where, without God, you could be in deep weeds.

In our application packet for aspiring missionaries, we ask the new applicants, "Are you able to stand alone in defense of the Scriptures or convictions?" Standing alone is difficult at best. In this story Shadrach, Meshach and Abednego had each other.

Leadership Life Principle #6: In the end times, expect the furnace to be heated up seventy-times-seven hotter. I believe we could potentially be living in the end times—not necessarily in the seven years of tribulation, but most likely in the birth pains as Jesus explained in Matthew 24. The disciples were quizzing Jesus as to when He might return initiating the beginning of the end of the age. Matthew 24 is a sobering chapter for those who have eternal security, but it is most frightening for those who do not. Speaking of the end of the age can spook even the most mature believer.

If we are living in the precursor to the end times, the birth pains, we need mature Christian leaders to lead. This is not a time to retreat but to charge forward. This is the stance that carried Shadrach, Meshach, and Abednego into the elite people of faith who knew God, loved God, and trusted in God. We need more of these kinds of people living today.

Summary

What's it going to take to increase your courage in living an outward life of conviction? There is a fine line between being respectfully heard and being too harsh. Being respectfully heard will create a meaningful conversation. Being an in-your-face, mega-phone, black and white personality will only cause a divisive debate, where neither side wins.

I have always endorsed the saying that you can say almost anything to anyone, if your tone of voice is not incendiary, demeaning, or belittling. As far as your style of communication, find your groove, find your lane, and stay in it. Being a Christian does not justify the world using you as a doormat. There will be times where you will need to stand up and declare your biblical convictions. Be prepared, your time is coming.

CHAPTER 6
CALEB - A MAN OF COURAGE

Caleb was a mighty warrior and a man of valor. Merriam-Webster's dictionary defines valor as the "strength of mind or spirit that enables a person to encounter danger with firmness: personal bravery."[3] Synonyms such as bravery, courage, fearlessness, courageousness, braveness, nerve, backbone, spine, heroism, audacity, boldness, gallantry, daring, spirit, fortitude, dauntlessness also describe a man of valor. All these qualities make up Caleb, one of my own personal heroes in the Bible. He is the kind of man I want to be.

There is a poem by Joshua Hudson that also speaks of valor:[4]

When dreadful times upon us fall
And evil scours the land
And men of weaker stature kneel
Men of valor stand

When darkness rises on each side
And day is choked by night

---

[3]*Merriam-Webster,* s.v. "valor," accessed August 12, 2020, https://www.merriam-webster.com/dictionary/ valor.
[4]Joshua Hudson, "Men Of Valor," Poem Hunter, accessed August 12, 2020, https://www.poemhunter.com/ poem/men-of-valor/.

And men who fear their lives concede
Men of valor fight

When all of hell is brought to bear
With every cruel intent
And all the common men have fled
With all their courage spent

And when all those who've made great boasts
Have turned their backs and run
You'll see the men of valor still
Their battle's just begun.

Standing until the end, whether you are standing for a physical battle or standing for truth—that is what valor is all about.

We read about Caleb in Numbers 13. Verses 1 and 2 state, "The LORD said to Moses, 'Send some men to explore the land of Canaan, *which I am giving* to the Israelites. From each ancestral tribe send one of its leaders'" (emphasis added).

God is God. He is all knowing. He didn't need a reconnaissance mission to make decisions or to assist Him in leading the nation into the Promised Land. That being said, I suspect this expedition was actually for the sake of Moses and the people, to encourage them by providing them with information as they prepared to go to war and take the land.

By this time, the nation of Israel had already experienced a number of God's miracles—they had lived through the plagues that infected Egypt and they had walked through a parted Red Sea! Now Moses was preparing these same people to enter into the Promised Land that God was giving to them. Like any other military strategist,

Moses naturally wanted enough data about the land first so he could then make wise, strategic decisions before the takeover. To do this, Numbers 13:17-20 says that Moses sent twelve spies—two being Caleb and Joshua—on a mission to collect information. He told them,

> Go up through the Negev and on into the hill country. See what the land is like and whether the people who live there are strong or weak, few or many. What kind of land do they live in? Is it good or bad? What kind of towns do they live in? Are they unwalled or fortified? How is the soil? Is it fertile or poor? Are there trees on it or not? Do your best to bring back some of the fruit of the land.

It's often overlooked that up until this point, Moses had followed the instructions of God without doing any further research like he was doing now; and except for his hesitating at the burning bush all those years ago, Moses had done everything that God had ever instructed him to do.

Scriptures tells us that the spies were in the land for forty days. This is significant because the number forty is mentioned in the Bible one hundred forty-six times, and it typically refers to a time of faith-testing, judgement, or probation. For example, during the time of Noah, it rained for forty days. Moses was on the mountain for forty days. The Israelites, too, had wandered the desert for forty years. And later, Jesus would be tested in the desert for forty days as well. Therefore, we might deduce that the forty days that the spies spent in the land was a testing time for them. The next verses in this chapter certainly makes it seem so.

Numbers 13 states that after forty days, the spies had gained firsthand knowledge of what the land produced.

Furthermore, Verse 23 says that they followed Moses' instructions to bring back some of the fruit: "When they reached the Valley of Eshcol, they cut off a branch bearing a single cluster of grapes. Two of them carried it on a pole between them, along with some pomegranates and figs." This evidence they carried back to Moses proved the land was productive and could sustain life. This is the report they brought back to Moses in verses 27-29:

> We went into the land to which you sent us, and it does flow with milk and honey! Here is its fruit. But the people who live there are powerful, and the cities are fortified and exceptionally large. We even saw descendants of Anak there. The Amalekites live in the Negev; the Hittites, Jebusites and Amorites live in the hill country; and the Canaanites live near the sea and along the Jordan.

Notice the exclamation mark after verse 27. We can assume that the spies came back fearful because of what they had seen. They were afraid that they would not be able conquer the land in their own strength. This fear, of course, reveals to us their underlying problem. Whenever we live life based on our own strength, and not on the promptings of the Almighty, we make bad decisions.

To illustrate we need only look at places of higher education around the world today. These colleges and universities share a goal of wanting to produce the next generation of critical thinkers. These critical thinkers are taught to look at data produced by scientists and researchers, and to make decisions according to the research. Inevitably, they also learn how to leave God out of the decision-making process. Throughout the COVID-19 pandemic crisis I have heard statements like, "The data shows—" or "the scientific data proves—" or "the anecdotal data does not prove—" made by intellectually-gifted people who are well-trained in their fields of study. However, we know that a person with a high intellect is not always necessary wise. If you've been following the news, perhaps you have realized that the process these intellectuals have been taught to use are not foolproof. How many times have we seen these men change their minds regarding COVID-19 protocol over the last few months? Thus, we can concede that a person with a university diploma or even with a high intellect is not always necessary wise.

Now please don't misread me—I too was trained in a university system, and I am a much better person for having successfully navigated through that higher educational system. However, it wasn't until years later when I learned to bring God into my decision-making process that I utterly understood what it was to be wise. I've learned that whenever we leave God out of our decisions, we end up making choices based on the wisdom of this world rather than the wisdom of God. Back in Numbers 13, we see our man Caleb rise up and address this problem in verse 30.

> Then Caleb silenced the people before Moses and said, "We should go up and take possession of the land, for *we can certainly do it*" (emphasis added).

> But the men who had gone up with him said, "We can't attack those people; they are stronger than we are." And they spread among the Israelites a bad report about the land they had explored. They said, "The land we explored devours those living in it. All the people saw there are great size. We saw the Nephilim there (the descendants of Anak come from the Nephilim). We seemed like grasshoppers

in our own eyes, and we looked the same to them" (vs. 31-33).

They continued in 14:2-4:

> "If only we had died in Egypt! Or in this desert! Why is the LORD bringing us to this land to only to let us fall by the sword?... Wouldn't it be better for us to go back to Egypt? And they said to each other, 'We should choose a leader and go back to Egypt."

What a great insult to the Lord who brought them out of captivity in the first place! And what folly to think their lives would be better if they went back to Egypt! Caleb, along with Joshua, once again try to address the problem by warning them, "Whatever you do, don't rebel against the LORD" (Num 14:9).

We know the rest of the story. The other ten spies got their way, and they managed to convince the people not to take the land, even though God already commanded Moses to destroy the entire nation. Moses pleaded with the Almighty on behalf of the people. God relented but pronounced a three-part judgement on the nation for their lack of faith in following through with His directives.

The first judgement was that not one person of the nation, twenty years or older would ever get to see the Promised Land except for Caleb and Joshua. The second judgment was that the nation would wander in the desert for forty years, one year for each day they spent spying out the territory. This meant that anyone twenty years or older would die off in the desert during those years. Think about that for a moment! Finally, the third judgment was a plague the Lord sent specifically to the ten spies and their families—the same ten who swayed the nation not to go in and take possession of the land.

That is the cost of NOT following the Lord as He instructs wholeheartedly. Sometimes death is the consequence of our disobedience. Other times it is not seeing what good and wonderful plan God had for your life. The ten spies experienced immediate death, while the nation experienced death over the forty years as they wandered the desert. They also suffered a loss in not seeing the Promised Land. Both losses were painful. I never want to experience either, simply because I had not fully followed His instructions.

On the flipside, Scripture shows us the results of obedience to God's word. I love how the Almighty describes Caleb in verse 24: "But because my servant Caleb has a different spirit and follows me wholeheartedly, I will bring him into the land he went to, and his descendants will inherit it." What a beautiful testimony of the Lord describing His servant.

It's worth noting that while I don't defend the spies' responses when they came back from their expedition, I do understand their concerns. I remember when Rhonda and I were invited to go on our first mission trip in 1999 to India, an extremely tough country for a first mission experience. I vividly remember coming out of the airport when we first landed, only to be met with strange sights and foreign smells. I recall weaving through the throngs of people for a half hour as we attempted to get to our taxis. It was unnerving! Unfamiliar people everywhere—people that were pushing, shoving, and grabbing. It was like walking through one of our regional festivals here in Seattle on a sunny day, only exponentially worse.

I remember almost everything about that trip and the many different unfamiliar situations we experienced. That is why I could possibly understand the spies' concerns when they returned from the Promised Land. When something is routine and known, it usually feels safe and comfortable. However, the unknown is scary and uncomfortable. The spies had lived in Egypt previously. Living in Egypt became routine and comfortable to them, even despite their oppression. Even after leaving Egypt, they had adjusted to living in the desert, their new routine and comfort. Like India had been to me and Rhonda, the Promised Land with its strange sights, smells, and people (some of whom were giants), must have looked very intimidating!

Considering all that God had done to deliver them from Egypt in the first place, that being said, it is still extremely odd that this was still their concluding attitude. Time after time, God had destroyed their enemies and spared them. He had sent ten plagues to afflict the Egyptians, but spared the Israelites in the process. He had parted the Red Sea so the Israelites could escape on dry land, flanked by walls of water, but had allowed those same waters to crash down on their enemies. I hope if I had seen those miracles firsthand, those displays of God's awesome power, I would be like Caleb and said, "We can do this—God will protect us again!"

Caleb was such a man of courage!

The problem comes when we forget the great things that God has done for us. I am reminded of this often, because at Prisoners For Christ, we are a faith ministry. This means we rely on the power of God to move on the hearts of our constituency to support the ministry financially. No year is ever guaranteed, and every year comes with financial issues that we pray for the Lord to solve. It seems that every summer, the donation levels drop significantly. Still, for over thirty years, God has provided. We need to remind ourselves of His faithfulness, but like the Israelites, we are often quick to forget.

Remember this: it is one thing to debate an issue, but it is something else to give into fear attempting to persuade people not to do something that God has instructed! That is what the ten spies did in their attempt to dissuade the nation. If you know you are in the will of God, fear not! Be a man or woman of courage.

What can we learn from the life of Caleb?

Leadership Life Principle #1: As a leader, dwell in the land of promises, not in the land of giants. To execute on that principle successfully, you need to know what those biblical promises are and identify what your land of giants looks like. That was a significant problem for the ten spies. They went. They observed. They reasoned. They feared.

Based on that fear, they made the horrendous decision to attempt to sway the nation away from the Lord's instructions—a decision that cost them their lives. Are you a man or woman of valor? If so, you must identify your land of giants. What are your giants? How are you going to overcome them? You must overcome any fear the enemy might send your way.

Leadership Life Principle #2: Understand words are extremely powerful—whether they are used for the positive or the negative. This is a principle that the ten spies did not understand, but Caleb did. James 3:5-6 says:

Likewise, the tongue is a small part of the body, but it makes great boast. Consider what a great forest is set on fire by a small spark. The tongue also is a fire, a world of evil among the parts of the body. It corrupts the whole body, sets the whole course of one's life on fire and is itself set on fire by hell.

Wow, what a powerful indictment against the tongue and words spoken carelessly. As a leader, purpose to build up and not to tear down. Be a man or woman of courage by keeping your words and mouth in check. Speak softly. If you are prone to sarcastic remarks, strive to reject any form of mean-spirited sarcasm directed toward anyone.

Leadership Life Principle #3: Don't allow yourself to be contaminated with stinking thinking. This is exactly what happened to the nation of Israel. They allowed ten men to dissuade them from executing God's perfect plan. It was decades ago when I heard the phrase "garbage in, garbage out." How true that statement still is today. If you constantly listen to bad news reports, you will become cynical and fearful of the future. If you listen to ungodly music, you will have ungodly thoughts. If you listen to the wrong crowd, you will start acting like them. Don't let the ungodly try to persuade you. As a leader in God's vineyard, you need to be wise, choosing what and who you listen to.

At the time of this writing, the world is in the grips of the COVID-19 pandemic. There are all sorts of bad news reports and conspiracy theories flying around social media, some of which are extremely deceptive. To illustrate, there is a dangerous new technology called "deep fake" which uses artificial intelligence (AI) to produce counterfeit videos. This allows a creator to make someone say something on a video that he or she has not said. These videos look seamless, with words matching perfectly to the speaker's mouth and in the speaker's voice. Just think about what could come out of a political figure's mouth with this kind of technology. In the hands of nefarious people, deep fake videos can light catastrophic fires on social media. Before you buy into any type of ideology or video messaging on social media, be careful. Don't allow stinking thinking to seep into the recesses of your mind. Be extremely careful in what you read and pray for discernment.

Leadership Life Principle #4: Realize some leaders remain resilient way beyond their years. Our man of this chapter, Caleb, is just that person. Look with me at Joshua 14:10-12:

> Now then, just as the LORD promised, he has kept me alive for forty-five years since the time he said this to Moses, while Israel moved about in the desert. So here I am today, eighty-five years old! I am still as strong today as the day Moses sent me out; I am just as vigorous to go out to battle now as I was then. Now give me this hill country that the LORD promised me that day. ... but the LORD helping me, I will drive them out just as He said.

Caleb was forty years old when he went to the Promised Land as one of the twelve spies. He spent the next forty years of his life wandering in the desert with the rest of the nation, and five years later, he had a conversation with his friend Joshua about his inheritance. He was old by then, yet his leadership qualities never wavered—that was Caleb. He confirms this in verse 12, when he says that he was as strong as he was when Moses sent him out. Additionally, his heart for the Lord was still evident in his old age, too.

Verse 12 says, "But the LORD helping me, I will drive them out just as I said." Leaders never stop leading even during trials. Caleb was undoubtedly a man of resilience.

Leadership Life Principle #5: Resolve to speak when the Holy Spirit prompts you to speak! This is a major takeaway of this story. I can see this young forty-year-old with fire in his eyes standing up in front of the assembly saying, "We should go up and take possession of the land, for we can certainly do it." It took resolve to do this, and we see that the ten spies' lack of faith was what caused their deaths. Contrarily, Joshua and Caleb lived because they put their trust in the Lord resolving to complete the task at hand. Despite the odds against them, they spoke up, and in the end they were blessed for that.

Leadership Life Principle #6: Commit to being a man or woman of courage. Caleb was refined in the refiner's fire, but sometimes, it is hard to be a lone voice. I have always said that as a leader, you can say almost anything to anybody if you have the right demeanor, tone of voice, are not rude, and don't react to personal attacks. Add to that list a humble spirit, and you can say just about anything.

Summary

What does it take to be a man or woman of courage? The courage stripes do not come easily and take time to be earned. Sometimes courage is also honed by planned determination, like in a military operation. Regardless of how you gain courage, know that courage is often demanded of you when you least expect it. It is demanded when you have the least amount of time to decide your course of action. Remember that when these moments come, do not react. Instead, respond.

This is what Caleb did. Play out some scenarios in your mind of past failures in how you might have muffed some high-octane communications. Start mentally preparing yourself for the next time you can show courage.

CHAPTER 7

GIDEON - A MAN WHO LISTENED TO THE VOICE OF GOD

I dare to say that most Christians want to hear from God and be touched by God in their daily walk; they want to know God's plan for their lives. However, most Christians have difficulty knowing what God's plan is for their lives. We don't have to go very far into the New Testament to read God's plan for our knowing His will. Romans 12:2 says, "Do not conform any longer to the pattern of this world, but be transformed by the *renewing of your mind.* Then you will be able to test and *approve what God's will is*— his good, pleasing and perfect will" (emphasis added). Faithful ones, it doesn't get much clearer than that. As believers, we need to strive to become more Christ-like in our daily walk. We need to grow closer to Him by the renewing of our minds.

To help us grow closer to Him, the Bible is replete with examples of men and women of God who faced insurmountable odds which caused them to tremble in their faith as the Almighty guided them in trusting Him. Gideon's story is one from which we can learn great lessons. It is one in how to learn to overcome your fear of doing great things for the Kingdom.

His story begins in Judges 6, where we once again read of Israel rebelling against God's statutes. As a result of their insolence, God sends a marauding army to oppress the nation. Knowing of Israel's agricultural economy, this Midianite army makes it difficult for the Israelites to grow and harvest any food. We learn that a man named Gideon—being an extremely resourceful man—uses the winepress not just as a winepress, but also as a threshing floor for wheat. It is in one of these dark moments on the threshing floor that the angel of the Lord appears to Gideon, instructing him to save Israel. The angel makes this pronouncement in verse 12, "The LORD is with you, mighty warrior."

The angel of the Lord's words "mighty warrior" confuses Gideon. It would have confused me as well if the angel had appeared to me. I know I am not a fighting man, and Gideon knew he wasn't either. It's conceivable that Gideon might have also been suffering from an inferiority complex because of his response in verse 15 saying, "My clan is the weakest in Manasseh, and I am the least in my family." What was Gideon saying in this verse? He was saying that he was a nobody—he had no position in life or in his family; he had no clout. He might have also been looked down upon by many in his tribe. He might not have been endowed with good looks or brain power. He might have been perceived as a bumbling klutz. His shortcomings may even have been thrown in his face by his parents or peers, with words such as, "You will never amount to anything." There could have been many reasons why he responded this way.

Have you ever felt out of place or inferior in your life journey? Have you ever felt unworthy to fulfil a certain role, or to do a specific task? If so, what can you do today about that fear that is holding you back from doing God's will?

What would you do for the Kingdom of God if you had no fear?

Who am I? What do I have to offer? Why should I believe that I can be a leader in the church or my community?—these are questions many Christians ask when they consider becoming leaders. Essentially, they felt the same way that Gideon felt. They might also think, *People who have gone to seminary or who have other training are the leaders in the church, but not someone like me.* Know that this is exactly where the enemy of God wants you to stay in life. He needs you to succumb to your fear so that you fail to fulfill God's plan for His Kingdom. But remember—fear is not of God. Fear renders the believer ineffective for the cause of Christ.

I often ask my leaders at Prisoners For Christ, "What would you do for the Kingdom of God if you had no fear?" Beloved, make a list on a piece of paper of your fears about being a leader. I know that some of you will think, *Why me, when there are others more qualified? I haven't been to seminary. I can't speak in front of people. I am not particularly good at leading. I am afraid of what people will think. I can't raise money. I can't preach or teach. I can't quit my job. I have no time. I am afraid of failing. What will my family think of me? What will my friends think? I stutter. I don't look the part. I may have a physical handicap or even a mental handicap.*

The excuses are endless.

I don't know how many items you wrote on your piece of paper, maybe it was three or maybe it was twenty. Whatever it was, do these next six things for me.

- First, ask yourself one more time, "What would I do for the Kingdom of God, if I had no fear?"
- Second, rip up that piece of paper and file it in the trash can.

- Third, offer yourself up as a living sacrifice unto the Lord.
- Fourth, say to the Lord, "Use me in whatever way you have called me."
- Fifth, wait on the Lord.
- Sixth, fast and pray for direction.

The world is becoming a darker and darker place for Christians. The church and this dying world need Christian leaders who can climb out on a limb to be used by God. Have you ever been out on a limb? Have you ever been so far out on a limb that it started to bend? This is exactly where God wants you—in a place where all your trust is in Him.

Where God calls, He equips!

I have good news for you. I have a 100% guarantee for you, if you will receive it. If you fall into the category of a Gideon, who had an inferiority complex, know this—where God calls, He equips. He did it for me and He will do it for you, too. He did it for Moses and He did it for Gideon. Hebrews 11 is full of examples of people whom He called and equipped. Fear not saints! Do not allow the enemy to persuade you any differently. Raise your hand and be counted. Volunteer in some capacity. Hang out with other leaders. Observe their strengths and observe their weaknesses.

In the story of Gideon, we notice a strange thing. If the angel of the Lord appeared to me and gave me instructions, that would be enough for me to start making tracks towards completing the mission. I suspect the same is true for you. For Gideon, however, this was not enough to convince him. He wanted signs to confirm that he was actually speaking to the Lord; he wanted proof of it. God obliged, and Gideon received four signs that confirmed his course of action, three of which he requested and one which he did not.

Verse 17 says, "If now I have found favor in your eyes, give me a sign, that it is really you talking to me." The angel then touched the tip of his staff to the meat and unleavened bread and fire flamed up, consuming the meat and unleavened bread. Following this, the angel disappeared. For most of us, this occurrence would have been enough proof that the Lord was indeed speaking.

Not for Gideon, however; he still needed more proof. He next asked for a fleece to be wet with dew on a dry ground (vs. 37). God answered by making the fleece sopping wet. Though trepidatious of God now, Gideon still asks God for a third sign. This time, he requests that the fleece be dry, while the ground is dewy. God once again shows himself by obliging this request.

The fourth sign, however, Gideon did not ask for. It was a "bonus" for Gideon. He was instructed to go into the camp of Midian at night. There he hears two soldiers talking about a dream one of them had. They interpret the dream to mean that God is handing the entire army into the hands of Gideon. Upon hearing this, Gideon is greatly encouraged. He worships God and then takes immediate action to ready his small army of just three hundred men.

This is a great story of God's miraculous hand being on His servant, Gideon. Gideon went from being a nobody to being a somebody in the army of God. He went from threshing wheat in the winepress to planning military strategies. Gideon's story will be discussed until the end of days.

If you are like me, perhaps you sometimes feel that you could never aspire to that form of leadership. Maybe you think that stories like these in the Bible apply only to biblical times but not for today. I'm here to say that your assessment is both right *and* wrong. You are correct that in your own strength and apart from God, you could never aspire to that level of leadership. But you are wrong to think that this kind of miraculous leadership was only for then. If God calls you, He will equip you. He will equip you just like he equipped Moses, who had a speech impediment, and like Gideon, who was a nobody.

God will meet you in your fear. He only requires one thing of you—faith. He doesn't even require you to take a full step forward. He simply requires you to move one foot, a quarter of an inch forward, in faith. That is progress. You may even need to grasp one of your legs with both hands to move that foot a quarter of an inch because you are so fearful, and that's okay. It is still progress. He will meet you amid your iniquity, as well as in your fear.

If you want to walk on the water, as Peter did, you need to get out of the boat. There were twelve disciples in that boat who were all terrified, but only one crawled out of the boat. Peter, like Gideon, asked Jesus for a sign. He said in Matthew 14:28, "Lord, if it's you, tell me to come to you on the water," and Jesus instructed him to, "Come."

There have been many sermons written about Peter's failing to not trust in the Lord fully as he was walking on water. However, I see it as a great victory for Peter because he took that first step and crawled out of the boat. That, in and of itself, is a great victory! Peter started walking on water, saw the storm, became fearful, took his focus off Jesus, and then began to sink. The takeaway for me is this: if I am called by God and I step out in faith, I know that He will reach out His hand to rescue me should I succumb to fear and begin to sink.

In the story of Peter walking on water, the boat represents safety, your comfort zone. If you want to walk on water, you must be willing to leave your perceived place of comfort and contentment. Is God calling you to get out of the boat? What is your boat? What needs to happen for you take that step of faith?

What can we learn from the life of Gideon?

Leadership Life Principle #1: Understand that God can use you despite your limitations. Over thirty five years ago, when I first began preaching in the jails and prisons, I often said to offenders, "God can still use you, no matter what your life circumstances might be at the present time." One night an inmate told me that he didn't believe me. He believed that people like himself were beyond spiritual redemption. He found it unfathomable that someone like him could ever be used by God in any fashion. It just so happened that my pastor at the time had just used an illustration in his sermon *Why God Shouldn't Hire Us*. In this sermon, he gave an illustration listing famous Bible characters who all had reasons that should have disqualified them from being used by God. I asked my pastor if I could have a copy to be used for inmates, and he happily obliged. I have reprinted it below.

- Moses stuttered
- David's armor didn't fit
- John Mark was rejected by Paul
- Hosea's wife was a prostitute
- Jacob was a liar
- David had an affair
- Solomon was too rich
- Abraham was too old
- David was too young

- John was self-righteous
- Naomi was a widow
- Rahab was a prostitute
- Moses and King David were murderers
- Jonah ran from God
- Miriam was a gossip
- Gideon and Thomas both doubted
- Jeremiah was depressed
- Elijah was burned out
- Martha was a worrywart
- Mary was lazy
- Samson had long hair
- Noah got drunk

There are lots of reasons why God shouldn't use us. But He'll use us despite who we are, where we've been, who we have hurt, or what we look like. Isn't it obvious that God deliberately chooses men and women that culture overlooks, exploits, and abuses?

He chooses the lowly things of life, the nobodies of this world, to expose the darkness of this world. Everything that we are and all that we have: right thinking, right living, a clean slate, and a fresh start comes from God by way of Jesus Christ. That's why we say if you are going to blow a horn, then blow a trumpet instead for the Lord.

That about sums it up. God is sovereign and will use whom He so chooses. The question for you as a leader is this: will you allow God to use you in mighty ways? Remember, to walk on water, you need to get out of your boat first.

The inmate who doubted that he could ever be used by God, asked me to send him that sermon illustration, and I did. I trust that he was encouraged and was able to get his life back on track. I never heard from him again.

Leadership Life Principle #2: Realize man looks at the outward appearance, but God looks at the heart. This principle goes hand-in-glove with Leadership Life Principle #1. In 1 Samuel 16:7 the Bible reads, as Samuel is at Jesse's house, "Do not consider his appearance or his height, for I have rejected him. The LORD does not look at things man looks at. Man looks at the outward appearance, but the LORD looks at the heart." In one of my training books on recruiting volunteers for prison ministry, I talked about my preconceived notions as to how volunteers should look. I was a young stockbroker and I had the mindset that all volunteers needed to dress more like I did. It took a thumping from the Lord after I knowingly rejected volunteers because they did not fit my particular mold. The Lord spoke firmly to me that I should not reject anyone that He sent to the ministry. That correction of my attitude started me down the path of heavy recruitment. Once I was totally repentant, the Lord opened the floodgates for new volunteers to join the forces of PFC.

Have you ever rejected anyone because of how he or she looked? Never reject someone because of the outward appearance for it may be that the Lord has placed that person in your path to help you achieve His plans for you.

Leadership Life Principle #3: God desires to help His servants increase their faith. Increasing our faith is not easy. It takes work. As I have often said, faith is like a muscle—the more you exercise it, the bigger it grows. We need to trust the Lord daily in all things, attempting to crawl further and further out on the limb of your faith walk. Hebrews 11:6 says, "And without faith it is impossible to please God." Oh, how I want to please God! It is my desire to please the Father and imagine Him smiling down at me. I want the Lord to look upon me as I look upon my children or grandchildren when I say to them, "You bring such great joy to me when I watch you." I want the Lord to be pleased with me. I am a man with clay feet, and I will make mistakes. I ask for forgiveness when I sin, but I want nothing more than to please the Lord of my life.

Leadership Life Principle #4: When God asks you to do something, don't make excuses. It is often human nature to reason away or to *overthink* decisions or actions that we believe have been directed by the Lord. *I am not ready. I can't do that. Is God really asking me to do this?*—these questions can easily take over our minds. Understand, I never endorse blind faith—which is running blindly off a two-thousand-foot cliff, expecting God to save you. I believe in seeking godly counsel. However, you need to remember that even people we look up to spiritually can get it wrong. The best we can do is compare what we hear from godly counselors and wait for a clearer direction from the Holy Spirit.

Summary

Gideon is one of my favorite people of the Bible. The angel of the Lord showed up unannounced one day and told Gideon he was a mighty warrior. Gideon listened, asked God for confirmations, and then took immediate action. He was a man who listened to that still small voice of the Lord. Are you like Gideon? Do you listen to that still small voice or do you ignore it? Do you make excuses? Do you become frustrated when you receive a prompting from the Spirit because it conflicts with the busyness of your daily tasks? To be a leader, you need to be sensitive to the voice of the Shepherd, our Commander in Chief. What must you do to be more available to the Spirit's leading? Remember, Gideon was a man who listened to the voice of God.

CHAPTER 8

JONATHAN - A MAN OF LOYALTY

Loyalty is one of my main core values. My closest friends and I have formed an unbreakable bond of loyalty over the years, meaning that we are loyal to each other. Nevertheless, if you are friend of mine, I am resolute to be loyal to you until the day one of us dies. If you need something of me at three in the morning, I'll be there for you in a nanosecond. And if you're one of my closest friends, then I know in my heart of hearts that you would reciprocate the action toward me also. I am blessed to have these relationships in my life that are built upon loyalty.

Loyalty is a funny thing, though. It is not like faith—which will grow the more you use it. I don't recall a day when I ever determined to become more loyal; neither do I have memory of ever being any more or less loyal than I am today. I've never tried to develop my loyalty into a stronger gift either. It has simply always been with me. Much like my two pinky fingers that have been with me since birth, so has my loyalty. And I suppose this is just the way God built me. I often muse that you can't take the moo out of the cow or the whinny out of the horse; some things are just inherent in how God designed us. Thus I count my loyalty as a true gift from God, and it is so much part of who I am that I can't even imagine what life is like for those who have no friends, since they have no one they can trust or be loyal to.

Similarly, I also have the gift of administration, something I realized early on in my business career. I have no problem staying organized and updated on paperwork. I even enjoy reading books that discuss organization and administrative skills. As I observe the world around me, many peers clearly do not enjoy this same gift. Just as many do not have loyalty, they lack the gift of administration, also.

For me, there were buddies from grade school, high school, and college who have remained my faithful friends throughout the years. Although we have taken different life paths, different career paths, and while we may even be on opposite sides of the political aisle, we are all still very loyal to one another. On the flipside, though, there are those who have betrayed me, too. It is an unfortunate fact of life that there will always be people who will let you down. The reality of such disappointments is that it is difficult to recover from the betrayal of a trusted friend.

Perhaps you too have experienced this intense emotional pain before, and maybe it has caused you to be extremely cautious of who you let into your life. While I understand your pain, my advice to you is to never give up on finding loyal friends. Furthermore, I advise you to consider remaining loyal to even those who have betrayed you. I say this because in my life, there are those people who are no longer part of my "inner core." These people have left our relationships in less-than-friendly ways. And though they have demonstrated a lack of loyalty, I still want to retain my loyalty to them. I dare say, that if they needed it, I would still travel the depths of the Sahara desert to rescue them. The point here is that if nothing changes for you (you being the one who was first betrayed), at least the offender will always have an opening of redeeming himself with you. The ball will be in their court. They will never be able to blame you for shutting them out. What a beautiful picture of what God is like with his sheep, who constantly wander off!

For these reasons, the story of Shadrach, Meshach, and Abednego has resonated with me since the very first time I read it. These three friends stayed the course, supporting each other, even during their worst trial—facing death by fire. One of them could have said, "If you guys are willing to die, then go for it. I am getting off the train now," but because of their strong devotion to the Lord and their strong bonds of friendship with each other, they stood together and fought the good fight. These three guys are my heroes! Furthermore, it's worth mentioning that Scripture also contains other admirable examples of loyalty—for example, Joshua's loyalty to Moses, and later, Jonathan's to David.

To fully understand the magnitude of the loyalty between Jonathan and David, one needs to understand first that Jonathan was the rightful heir to the throne upon the death of his father, King Saul. Yet, Jonathan still developed a brother-like relationship with David, whom God had ordained to be the next king of Israel instead. The Bible tells us about the depth of this friendship in 1 Samuel 18:1 saying, "Jonathan became one in spirit with David." We read in verse 4 that "Jonathan took off the robe he was wearing and gave it to David, along with his tunic, and even his sword, his bow and his belt." When David and Jonathan met, they immediately developed a close friendship. This is one of the closest friendships chronicled in the Bible. These two best friends didn't allow any problems or even family issues to interfere with their friendship—even when his own father began hunting David down.

You see, Jonathan not only had loyalty, but had his loyalties prioritized. He was first loyal to the Lord, then to his father Saul and his friend David. Therefore, when Jonathan found himself caught between two of the most important people in his life—his father Saul and David—he had a decision to make. His father Saul wanted to kill David, who was chosen by God to be Israel's next ruler. What was Jonathan to do? With whom would his ultimate loyalties lie? Jonathan knew that his father was irrational and had murder in his heart towards David. Therefore, he decided to protect David. Samuel 19:1-2 states, "Saul told his son Jonathan and all the attendants to kill David. But Jonathan was very fond of David and warned him, 'My father Saul is looking for a chance to kill you.'"

Furthermore, Chapter 20 tells of another time when Jonathan protected David from Saul's murderous intent. Jonathan did this by shooting arrows beyond David and instructing a servant boy to fetch the arrows beyond that spot. This was a prearranged signal from Jonathan to David that he needed to run for his life. Jonathan was indeed a man of loyalty!

As we focus on this topic for the remainder of this chapter, it's also important to know that there are four different types of loyalty.

- First, there is loyalty between friends as seen with Shadrach, Meshach and Abednego going into the fiery furnace together.
- Second, there is loyalty between bosses and employees, as seen between Joshua and Moses.
- Third, there is loyalty to an organization.
- Fourth, there is loyalty to an ideology or cause, as seen in the men who took a vow not to eat anything until they had killed the Apostle Paul (Acts 23:12-24)

Should loyalty ever end?

We need to ask the question, "Should loyalty ever end?" And if it should, when should that happen? Where does loyalty begin and where does it end?

Loyalty starts with the beginning seeds of trust between two individuals. As friendship and trust are developed between them over time, the level of loyalty forms thicker strands of strength. However, if someone in the relationship becomes manipulative or abusive, that's when the pause button should be pushed, until matters can be resolved.

Thus, loyalty can end when someone asks another to overlook sin for sake of saving face or side-stepping the natural consequences of that sin. However, the act of sweeping sin underneath the carpet never ends well; it only delays the inevitable and destroys relationships. You may even find that being part of this kind of deception can demolish your own reputation once everything is eventually revealed. At which point you will be at risk of losing other friends over withholding pertinent information. Trust me, I have seen this happen; it's undeniable that overlooking sin rips friendships apart.

To illustrate this concept, let's play out a scenario. Let's say you were given firsthand knowledge (not hearsay) that a close friend—to whom you were loyal—was about to enter into an adulterous relationship. Let's say you were asked not to tell anyone about it. This would be an example of when your loyalty should change its course. The swift hand of accountability begins with tough love.

Let me be clear—in a situation like the one above, you are not ending the friendship with your friend, but you are temporarily pausing loyalty between the two of you. As difficult as it may be for you to let go of that loyalty, you must realize that in these kinds of situations, you may be the only one who could prevent your friend from diving head first into a destructive lifestyle. This is *not* the time to bail on your friend! If you should ever be in a position such as this, understand that God in His sovereign will has allowed you to be in that position for His reasons. He has raised you up for such a time as this.

Let's look at another example. Let's say you have a friend with a gambling addiction, and you find out that he's been at the casino. You confront him about it, but he asks you not to tell his wife. What would you do? First, be prepared for your friend to lash out at you. Comments such as, "Don't judge me, you hypocrite!" "What about the time I did this for you?" "You are no friend of mine!" "I hate you!" "I never want to see you again!" "Get out of my life." "I will do what I want to do, when I want to, and you have no say." Venomous words like these can cut deep; they can make your head swim. They may even cause you to doubt your friendship ever existed! Furthermore, it can take time to heal after such a verbal attack, time in which you may begin doubting how loyal you now feel toward your friend.

However, think of it this way—even though your loyalty might seem to wane in these times of conflict, it really is not declining. In fact, it's probably growing stronger. It is sad to note that you will probably be the only one to notice this during this time! It takes a strong individual with strong friendship ties to stay the course with someone who is hurling such vitriol at you. Never give up on a friend who is in a sin crisis until Matthew 18 has fully run its course.

> If your brother sins against you, go and show him his fault, just between the two of you. If he listens to you, you have won your brother over. But if he will not listen, take one or two others along, so that

every matter may be established by the testimony of two or three witnesses. If he refuses to listen to them, tell it to the church; and if he refuses to listen even to the church, treat him as you would a pagan or a tax collector (Matt 18:15-17).

At this point, naturally your friendship changes. Instead of an outward friendship, you have what I call a prayer closet friendship. This means that you are on your knees travailing in prayer for your friend in your quiet time. Your friend may not know it, but you and the Lord know it.

Hence, this is what makes up much of life—messy issues with flawed people. How are you going to react when confronted with these kinds of loyalty issues?

Jonathan was a great friend to David. One could say Jonathan saved David's life by informing him of Saul's plan to kill him. But what if Jonathan had been alive when David was considering his affair with Bathsheba? What do you think he would he have said to David? How would he have attempted to intervene, or would he even have attempted to intervene at all? Confronting a king in these days was no minor feat—a man could be killed for doing that! Would Jonathan's friendship with David have survived a confrontation like this about the affair, or about the subsequent murder plot of Bathsheba's husband? We read in Scripture the prophet Nathan was the only one who intervened and confronted David. This happened after the sin had transpired, and only after prompting from God.

Do you have loyal friends? How are you going to nurture those relationships with those friends so that they become as strong as the friendships of Shadrach, Meshach, and Abednego? Is making friends hard for you? Pray for the Lord to bring men or women into your life with whom you can form intimate, trustworthy relationships.

What can we learn from the life of Jonathan?

Leadership Life Principle #1: Understand we were created to be in relationship with God first and others second. That is first and foremost. As leaders we must understand that we were ultimately created to be in fellowship with our Creator. If we can't get that right, how do we expect to get other relationships correct?

Leadership Life Principle #2: Understand loyalty is a two-way street. I often hear people say that their relationship seems one-sided, meaning they feel like all they are doing is pouring time and energy into another person's life, while getting nothing in return.

If you are in a relationship like that, it may seem as if the other person is very needy, sucking the life blood out of you. If this is the case, it is all about your perspective. You need to change your perspective. Recognize the relationship for what it is. Realize that this relationship is not based on loyalty, but on a discipleship relationship. They need mentoring. You are the mentor and they are the mentee.

Once you realize this, your entire outlook on that friendship will change. If you were previously looking to this person for a loyal friendship but instead found yourself in a discipleship relationship, then you probably feel like the relationship has not met your expectations. Know that there is nothing wrong with that, but now you will need to adjust your expectations. Furthermore, if you are still looking for a loyal friend who can provide you with give-and-take relationship, you may have to look elsewhere.

Leadership Life Principle #3: Understand to be in a loyal relationship both parties must be transparent. A relationship between two friends may consist of two peers of equal Christian maturity and loyal to one another. However, sometimes in such relationships, one might fail to be as transparent as the other, and this can potentially cause issues for the relationship. The good news is that it is usually an easily rectifiable situation; a simple talk about transparency can change much. If it doesn't, then that spotlights the nature of that relationship.

The truth is many people have an easier time being loyal than they do being transparent. While there are many reasons for why people lack transparency, the most common has to do with trust or a lack of trust. It happens when one party doesn't trust the other party to keep matters confidential. Another common reason for a lack of transparency is that many people fear showing others their inner selves. Don't forget, though, that fear is rooted in pride.

First, people lack transparency when they lack trust, and this often happens because they have been burned in the past by so-called friends who didn't keep personal matters confidential. When a friend breaks trust by spreading around confidential information, it causes great pain for all parties. For those of us who have been around prison ministry for some time, we understand confidentiality. There is a high price to be paid for breaking confidence in a prison setting.

Second, we often lack transparency when we fear showing our true selves. Some even liken transparency to standing in their front window in their birthday suit, and I get that! This fear of transparency is understandable, especially if you are not used to being transparent. Furthermore, it is much easier to be transparent with one person than it is to be transparent with a group of people, therefore making this task of transparency even more difficult for leaders.

Summary

Jonathan was a great friend to David, and there is much we can learn about loyalty from their relationship. When I get to Heaven, as much as I want to meet David, I really want to hang out with Jonathan. I want to see what made him tick, because he was a man of loyalty. I believe we can all learn lessons from the life of Jonathan. As we grow in our leadership skills, let us purpose to find those people whom we can trust to be part of our inner circle of loyal co-laborers.

CHAPTER 9
DAVID - A MAN OF STRATEGIC PLANNING

No other person in the Bible is more notably referenced as a military strategist than King David. He was brilliant in dealing with his adversaries. We first see this demonstrated when David sells himself to Saul as being the chosen one to attack the giant, Goliath. As he presents his qualifications to fight Goliath in 1 Samuel 17:34-37, we read about David's victories as a shepherd by killing both a lion and a bear to protect the sheep.

In David's younger years, the Lord was maturing him to be a military strategist. Verse 40 says that David collected five stones as he was preparing to fight Goliath with his sling. Why did he pick five stones? Did he doubt God could assist him in killing Goliath with only one stone? I think not. Did he think he might miss? I think not. David had already killed a lion and bear with the laser accuracy of his sling!

Rather, I believe that David understood the culture of the time, and the five stones meant he was prepared for blood revenge. This occurred when a relative of someone who was killed exacts revenge on the one who killed that relative. David knew Goliath had four brothers. He picked up an additional four stones, in preparation to fight the other brothers, if necessary. This is the first example of David being a strategic military strategists at a young age.

The next example comes in the next chapter, when Saul requires David to bring back one hundred foreskins of their Philistine enemies. This is Saul's price for David to marry one of Saul's daughters. Rather than bringing one hundred back, 1 Samuel 18:27 tells us that David was an overachiever and his soldiers killed two hundred Philistines instead. Of course, this killing could not have occurred without strategic military planning.

One of the more bizarre strategic moves occurred when David fled from Saul to King Achish in Gath.

> That day David fled from Saul and went to Achish king of Gath. But the servants of Achish said to him, "Isn't this David, the king of the land? Isn't he the one they sing about in their dances:
>
> 'Saul has slain his thousands, and David his tens of thousands.'"
>
> David took these words to heart and was very much afraid of Achish king of Gath. So, he pretended to be insane in their presence; and while he was in their hands he acted like a madman, making marks on the doors of the gate, and letting saliva run down his beard (1 Sam 21:10-13).

I have always laughed at the image of this great and mighty warrior—the warrior who had killed Goliath—faking his own insanity. However, this was yet another strategic move on David's part because we see, in 1 Samuel 22:1, David escaping.

Thus, David was a strategic thinker, and he remained a strategic thinker throughout 1 Samuel as he ran from Saul. David had his band of followers, and together they went on many raids to survive. This all took strategic planning; he never went halfcocked. Furthermore, the Lord was with David and fought his battles for him. It is worth noting here that many times when David planned a raid to do battle, he inquired of God—something he is still known for doing even today. Because of David's inquiring of God, the Bible even describes him as a man after God's own heart.

Then as we move to 2 Samuel, we observe the rebellion of David's son, Absalom, who wanted to take over the Kingdom. 2 Samuel 15:13-14 describes the situation:

> A messenger came and told David, "The hearts of the men of Israel are with Absalom." Then David said to his officials who were with him in Jerusalem, "Come! We must flee, or none of us will escape from Absalom. We must leave immediately, or he will move quickly to overtake us and bring ruin upon us and put the city to the sword."

For the sake of his family, servants, and the greater good of the citizens of Jerusalem, David decided to leave immediately, likely to avert civil war and further bloodshed. In 2 Samuel 15:25-28, David made strategic plans as he was in the act of fleeing. He instructed Zadok, who was a Levitical priest and was leading the procession of the Ark, to go back to the city. David told Zadok to keep him informed about what Absalom was doing within the city.

We then observe a discussion between David and Hushai, in verses 2 Samuel 15:33-34. Hushai may have been elderly or a sick person because David says, "If you go with me, you *will be a burden to me*. But if you return to the city and say to Absalom, 'I will be your servant, O king; I was your father's servant in the past, but now I will be your servant,' then you can help me by frustrating Ahithophel's advice" (emphasis added). This shows David employing counter-intelligence measures in a crisis.

This ploy seems to play out in Chapter 17. Absalom sought advice from Ahithophel (vs. 1-4). Absalom then decided to bring in Hushai for a second opinion (vs. 5). Hushai intentionally contradicted the advice of Ahithophel and Absalom took the bait. This "disinformation campaign" warned David of the coming doom, allowing him to escape one more time and ultimately allowing Joab, David's commander, to kill Absalom.

It is incontestable that David was an extremely wise, military strategic thinker. Though this chapter could have been titled many different ways that would have aptly described David, I believe one of his strongest suits was his ability to reason strategically. While he is known today for many of the great things he did in his lifetime I remember David as a brilliant strategist.

I believe leaders today need to be strategic thinkers, too. Of course, unless we have served in a branch of the armed forces, most of us will never be military strategists. There are, however, other ways we can be strategists. Furthermore, because we live in a rapidly changing world, leaders need to have that strategic mindset of being forward-thinking.

I remember a decade ago when I was in discussion with some *tech geeks*; they told me that technology was doubling every three years. We all marveled at that stat. That three-year-doubling effect has increased exponentially less than ten years later.

Buckminster Fuller created the "Knowledge Doubling Curve"; he noticed that until 1900 human knowledge doubled approximately every century. By the end of World War II knowledge was doubling every 25 years. Today things are not as simple as different types of knowledge have different rates of growth. For example, nanotechnology knowledge is doubling every two years and clinical knowledge every 18 months. But on average human knowledge is doubling every 13 months. According to IBM, the build out of the "internet of things" will lead to the doubling of knowledge every 12 hours.[5]

I am amazed that each doubling of knowledge took one hundred years until we reached the 1900s. That seems like a long time to me. By the end of the WWII, knowledge was doubling every twenty-five years. Some believe when Artificial Intelligence (AI) comes into full bloom, knowledge could double every twelve hours. How is that even possible? Or more importantly, what does that mean to church leaders or to those who lead Christian ministries? We need to understand, absent the speedy return of our Savior, change is occurring rapidly. If we are not nimble, flexible, and able to pivot when needed, we are going to get *run over*, running the risk of becoming obsolete.

In addition to the rapid changes that the exponential growth of knowledge continuously brings, unexpected worldwide crises tend to create even more shifts in our

---

[5]David Russell Schilling, "Knowledge Doubling Every 12 Months, Soon to Be Every 12 Hours," *Industry Tap*, June 13, 2017, https://www.industrytap.com/knowledge-doubling-every-12-months-soon-to-be-every-12-hours/3950.

world. Currently, the COVID-19 pandemic has dramatically changed everyone's way of life. Less than three months into 2020, most of the world went into quarantine and lockdown. Churches stopped services, schools closed, businesses stopped operating. When 2020 began, I could never have imagined how much our whole way of life would change in such a short amount of time. I never thought it was possible that the jails and prisons in the world would all close to volunteers in the same span of time—all of them!

Furthermore, we have seen major companies go out of business because of their failure to understand the impact that the internet would have on consumers and the way people buy goods. JC Penny, Sears, J Crew, Neiman Marcus, Gold's Gym, Pier 1 Imports, Hertz, GNC, Party City, Rite Aid, and Forever 21 represent just some of the major companies that have filed for bankruptcy or that are in significant financial trouble.

Twelve weeks ago, I had never attended a web-based video conference meeting, but now I attend meetings like this multiple times each week. Churches are holding online services. Schools are holding online classes. How does this tectonic shift impact the pre-COVID-19 evangelists, preachers, or teachers of the world? The new phrase in Christendom is *digital missionaries*. Do a web search on digital missionaries and you will find pages and pages of information on this topic.

In April of this year, I put out an email to our constituency telling them that I was putting together a Prisoners For Christ *Think Tank Team*, whose purpose was to think about the ministry's future in a COVID-19-impacted world. I wanted the group to answer several questions: What changes do we as a ministry need to make if the prisons remain closed for any length of time? What does ministry look like after the pandemic is over? How does Prisoners For Christ, if necessary, pivot? What does that pivot look like?

The reality is that all organizations on the face of this planet have four possible streams of revenue: 1) Companies sell products, 2) Companies sell services, 3) Governments, large and small, have the ability to collect taxes, and 4) Churches pass around offering plates.

Faith based organizations like PFC do not have any of those four opportunities for raising capital. Raising money for a Christian non-profit is already daunting, but raising donations for the cause of prisoners is even more challenging. As the president and the sole fundraiser for PFC, I must ask the tough questions. How is raising capital for the ministry going to change post-COVID-19? For the past thirty years, I have used only one strategy—build relationships, be humble, present the need, and then ask people to join in. Now, however, that strategy may be called old school. While I'll always believe in the power of building relationships, being humble, and presenting the needs necessary to run a ministry, we still must ask ourselves, "What about the *methodology* of doing all those things? How will that all change?"

I share this with you—not as a subtle method for asking for funds for PFC—but to present the idea that to be a leader today, you must think strategically. If you are a leader today, you must be asking yourself, "How is ministry going to change post-COVID-19? What must we do to pivot?" And more importantly than that, you need to think about what you'll do when the next COVID-19 pandemic or 9/11 type-of-crisis hits.

To illustrate the importance of asking these questions, consider this: When the automobile became accessible to the masses, the buggy whip manufacturers that didn't ask these kinds of questions went out of business. When the telephone was invented, the telegraph companies that didn't ask these questions went out of business. When washing machines were invented, the washboard companies that didn't ask these questions went out of business. The list is endless as technology evolves. The same phenomenon continues today, but on a much larger scale.

As leaders of churches and ministries, we must ask these same tough questions as technology changes. What must we do to change our mode of operation to remain viable? Do not get me wrong! The Gospel message of salvation never changes. However, at what point should methodologies change? Now, more than ever, we must be strategic thinkers and ponder these things.

What can we learn from the life of David?

Leadership Life Principle #1: Purpose to become a strategic thinker. When I was in high school, a friend invited me over and pulled out a chess board. I knew about the game of chess but found it overwhelming to learn all the moves assigned to each piece. However, all my friend wanted to do was play chess. He slaughtered me for the first twenty to thirty matches until I started to catch on to his strategies and began winning matches myself. Never thinking I was good enough, however, I never joined the high school chess team. After high school, I went on to college and joined a fraternity. I thought I could use my newfound chess prowess to really "show these frat boys." Boy, was I wrong! I was competing with those who were at a much higher skill level and I found myself getting completely annihilated.

Thus any free time I had was consumed with playing chess, until one day I was introduced to the game of Risk. My fraternity brothers and I began playing Risk for hours and hours. I tell you this because I genuinely believe that these two games developed my skills as a strategic thinker. Chess taught me to think four to five moves ahead; Risk taught me strategy development and to not spread myself too thin.

My advice to leaders at all levels is find ways to teach yourself how to become a strategic thinker. I would go so far as suggesting that you play chess or Risk with the young adults in your household. I would also suggest you develop your own think tank. Pull together a handful of people who can meet on a regular basis to resolve different issues. Be careful not to surround yourself with *yes* people. Also, be careful of adding staff to this think tank. They may not feel that they have the freedom to speak honestly. I have written a whole section on think tanks and advisory councils in one of my recent prison ministry training books called, *Prison Ministry Training, Advanced Series, Part 5*. If you have staff who report to you, feel free to add them, but add more non-staffers to your team who do not have an employee relationship with you.

Leadership Life Principle #2: Learn to inquire of the Lord about any new idea or direction. David became an expert at inquiring of the Lord. The Bible records nine different times where David inquired of the Lord (1 Sam 23:1-3, 4-5, 10-11, 12-14, 30:8-9; 2 Sam 2:1-2, 5:17-21, 22-25, 21:1). Of these nine inquiries, seven of them were over potentially life-threatening military campaigns and two were personal. All of these inquires had a positive outcome for David. However, they could have had disastrous outcomes had David not inquired of the Lord and if he had relied on his own strength. As leaders, I believe we need to be more in tune with the works of the Holy Spirit in our lives. We need to ask and inquire if the direction we are going is the will of the Lord for our lives.

Sometimes the reason we don't inquire of God is because we think we know better. Universities of the world train people to analyze data. Based on the findings of that data, decisions are made to pursue one direction over another. What happens when sound business analysis collides with the will of God? Disasters occur and stories of failure are written.

In today's fast paced, highly technological world, inquiring of the Lord is perceived as old school. However, it is far from old school. It is cutting edge technology that never changes. As leaders, we need to listen and act upon that still small voice that is always there, if we would only slow down and listen.

Leadership Life Principle #3: Realize to be a leader today requires courage. We are living in an ever-darkening world. This world and the people of this world are God-haters. They don't want anything to do with a loving God. It is as if we are living in the days of Noah.

I believe we are currently living in the birth pangs that Jesus spoke about in Matthew 24:4-8. This is a precursor to the ushering in of the Seven-Year Tribulation, the Year of the Lord, also known as the time of Jacob's Trouble. In my opinion, we are right there at the precipice. I believe Christ's return to rapture His church out of this world could occur at any time. I also know millions of people over the centuries have felt the same way—people who have lived through other catastrophic events like the Black Plague and the World Wars.

However, I believe the Lord's return is imminent for three prophetic reasons: First, there is the parable of the fig tree in Matthew 24:32-35. Many scholars believe this prophetic scripture set the time clock in 1948 with Israel once again becoming a nation. Second, there is the current regathering of the Jews from around the world, fulfilling the prophecy in Jeremiah 16:14-15 and Jeremiah 23:7-8. Third, there is the resurrection of the Hebrew language in Zephaniah 3:9. These are all miracles that have occurred in fulfillment of biblical prophecy in our lifetime.

For several years now, I have been posting on social media that if you want to know what time it is on the prophetic clock, you need only watch Israel. There has never been any nation in world like Israel. Despite being scattered throughout the world losing its homeland, Israel has also recovered it and has even resurrected its own dead language. It is in these dark, modern times that we see Israel fulfilling the Scriptures' on the end times. All this to say, it is this author's belief that the events in the world are NOT going to get any better. In fact, they are going to get much, much worse. We need leaders who are fearless and courageous. We can learn much from the life of David

Summary

David was many things, but he is most notably remembered for being a man after God's own heart. This is how I—like many others—have first come to know David. However, as outlined in this chapter, I now know David as a strategic thinker, too. If you are a leader in today's socioeconomic environment, you too must become a strategic thinker. Perhaps you have never thought of yourself as a strategic thinker. Now is the time to reevaluate that concept. Times are changing ever so rapidly. If you are not a strategic thinker, you and your organization may get run over. What must happen for you to become a strategic thinker?

CHAPTER 10

ELEAZAR - A MAN WHO WOULD NOT RETREAT

There are several Eleazars listed in the Bible, but the one whom I claim as one of my heroes is mentioned only once in the Bible, over two verses. The story of this Eleazar captivated me from the first time I read it, and it made me ask myself, "What kind of man does what he did?"

Consequently, I have tried to dig deeper into Eleazar's life over the years, but I have found there is not much known about him—a fact that does not alter the reality that his one story provides us with endless life lessons. These lessons are broad and pointed all at the same time. They may reach a variety of different people in different stages of life. I once prepared a sermon on Eleazar for inmates which inspired much discussion afterward; the men seemed to respond extremely well to this message. Likewise, the lessons we learn from Eleazar can also help us grow our leadership traits as administrators, also.

Eleazar's story comes shortly after Saul and Jonathan's deaths (2 Sam 21:14). We learn that David had several skirmishes with Israel's arch enemy, the Philistines (2 Sam 21:15-22). Chapters 22 and 23 then tells us about David's mighty men of valor which consisted of two groups—the thirty men listed in 2 Samuel 23:24-39, and three additional ones who were especially known for their great exploits. To put it into our common vernacular of today—if we were to classify David's thirty mighty men as Seal Team Six (the elite fighting arm of the Navy), then the three additional warriors would have to be in another class of their very own. They were *that* mighty!

The story picks up in 2 Samuel 23:8 which describes these three men: "Josheb-Basshebeth, a Tahkemonite, was the chief of the Three; he raised his spear against eight hundred men, whom he killed in one encounter." Wow! What kind of mighty war machine like this man could kill a trained army of eight hundred? The next verses then tells us about Eleazar.

> Next to him was Eleazar son of Dodai the Ahohite. As one of the three mighty men, he was with David when they taunted the Philistines gathered at Pas Dammim for battle. Then the men of Israel retreated, but he stood his ground and struck down the Philistines till his had grew tired and froze to the sword. The LORD brought about a great victory that day. The troops returned to Eleazar, but only to strip the dead (2 Sam 23:9-10).

That's it—those are the two verses which contain all that is known of Eleazar. In this two-verse short story, however, we learn that the army of Israel had originally gone to the front lines to fight, but then retreated, leaving Eleazar alone to fight. I can only imagine what was going through Eleazar's mind as he watched the rest of the troops fleeing. It was in those moments, he had to make a decision—would he retreat, or would he stand his ground?

Have you ever had to make a split-second decision like that? Maybe your experience with that was not as dramatic as a military battle. Maybe it was in some lesser degree, within your home or work life. Regardless of what your circumstances were, I'm sure it was nonetheless an uncomfortable decision to have to make.

The universal truth of this story is that it is always much easier to retreat than it is to stay and fight alone. This tendency of human nature is what makes me fear for Christians in a world that seems to have gone stark raving mad. Too often, Christians use the excuse that someone else is better equipped to fight the battle. Too many retreat from the battlefield to pursue lives of leisure, and thus Christians are failing miserably to engage the culture around them.

What then is the solution to this problem? It is that we need strong Christian leaders to run for political office so that we can change the course of our local communities, our states, and our federal government; we need more millennials to run for political offices; and lastly, we need more Christian judges on the benches.

Scripture states that Eleazar decided to stay and fight. When the fighting was over, his hand had frozen to the sword. Think about that for a moment, he fought so hard and for so long that his hand actually fused to his sword! Imagine if it had been your job to pry Eleazar's fingers from that sword; imagine the pain it must have caused him to unbend each of his fingers from the sword. In those moments you would certainly see firsthand (no pun intended) of Eleazar's commitment. And that, my friend, was *total* commitment.

I would be remiss here if I did not mention that there is a New Testament application to Eleazar's hand freezing to the sword. Let's look at the full armor of God in Ephesians 6:17 which states, "Take the helmet of salvation and the sword of the Spirit, which is the word of God." The sword was the weapon of combat of Eleazar's day, he had grasped it so hard for so long that he suffered for it. Similarly, today Christians need to engage in the culture wars and grab hold of *our* sword—the Word of God. We must do this with the same passion that Eleazar used when he grabbed hold of his physical sword.

But what would cause a person to choose to stay in the battle, even after he is completely spent? It is an undying commitment to a worthy cause. What cause are you willing to take up with that same fervor? And are you willing to give that cause your all, like Eleazar did?

In the late eighties, our church in Washington called for a peaceful protest for the protection of the unborn. I remember standing in line, shoulder to shoulder, on a sidewalk that stretched over six miles from the city of Kirkland all the way to the city of Bellevue. We protested twice. We believed that we were making a difference. So why did that protesting stop? Why does anything stop? And does it even make a difference? Thirty years after *Roe v. Wade* and over sixty million abortions later, abortions are still happening in alarming numbers in the United States.

Please let me indulge myself here and pontificate. Christians in America tend to live in the here and now. Many American Christians are uninformed about where the actual war is being waged. Instead of fighting for the right person to sit as president of the United States, we instead need to fight to take back control of the Supreme Court. Do we even know how to make the right decision when voting? When voting for the next president you must vote your values. I ask myself the following questions:

1. Which political party will best fight to protect my rights for religious freedom?

2. Which political party will best fight to protect the rights of the unborn child?

3. Which political party will best fight to protect Israel?

4. Which political party will best fight for the sanctity of marriage as one man to one woman?

5. Which political party will best fight to place a justice on the Supreme Court who aligns with my values?

Those are my five main core values. When I vote, I vote my values. The answers to those five questions are unmistakably clear to me. Christians need to do a better job in educating themselves and in considering what is at stake.

Why did the great movement of the Promise Keepers movement fizzle out? They had been an organization that was effecting change in the lives of men across this country in the nineties. It was a movement that was gaining momentum and that could have had major impact on generations ahead, but instead, it imploded. Why do organizations like Promise Keepers implode, and other organizations, like the Billy Graham Organization, grow? Let me give you three reasons.

1. **As John Maxwell once said, "Everything rises and falls on leadership."** Somehow, the leadership at the top loses its way. This happens when there is none at the top like Eleazar to stay the course of time to keep the ministry on track.

2. **Pride comes before the fall.** In the case of the Promise Keepers, I suspect there was a lot of fighting that

happened when it came time to adjust strategies, splintering the team. The quick rise of Promise Keepers may also have led those at the top to pride, with no checks and balances in place to prevent that from happening. I dare say that the imploding of the Promise Keepers was one of Satan's great victories of the last half century.

3. **They failed to pivot.** Promise Keepers became the Christian Sears and Roebuck of their time. They failed to understand the changing norms within our society. Finances started to decrease. Layoffs occurred. The uncontrolled death spiral began.

Failing to pivot is a catastrophic and seismic event—a business cancer that metastasizes. Once an organization begins that death spiral, it is living off life support. No organization that fails to PIVOT is exempt from the death spiral, and that means churches or non-profits alike. Society changes so fast that one must be nimble to survive. It saddens me greatly that this great movement fell by the wayside. Our country is sorely lacking good men to be fathers and heads of their households. This lack of fatherhood is one of the main reasons our generation is seeing a demise of the family and ultimately our country.

What ever happened to Myspace, the social media platform that was so popular in the early 2000s? It was sold in 2005 for $580 million. A mere three years later, it was in the death spiral, on life support, and was never able to recover. Facebook had become much more popular by then, and before we knew it, it had rendered Myspace obsolete. But what ultimately caused Myspace's failure, and why wasn't it able to recover? Why are other failing companies unable to recover?

Management gurus can dissect these massive business failures and come up with a whole host of reasons as to why these organizations have failed. One of those reasons usually involve the massive amounts of debt these companies typically accumulate before their demise. I have read such articles that say so and agree in part with some of their assumptions. I believe, however, that the primary reason why many companies die is that they fail to PIVOT. The more debt one has, the harder it is to PIVOT.

Let's get back to Eleazar. He was a man who was willing to lay down his life for a cause. He stayed the course. Some of the failing or failed organizations I have mentioned did not have this kind of dedicated leadership at the top. Many of their founders sold out for a hefty sum; others were forced out. When a company loses its visionary, it often loses the driving force needed to continue moving to the next level of growth. To effect change, you must buy into a cause for the long term, even without knowing the outcome.

What can we learn from the life of Eleazar?

Leadership Life Principle #1: As a leader, stay the course when the going gets tough. We need to always remember Romans 11:29 which states, "For God's gifts and his call are irrevocable." God doesn't make mistakes. If He has called you, He will provide the necessary means you need to get the job done. Why did God call me to head up a prison ministry in the early nineties when I had never been arrested? God's ways are truly not our ways! If we are the Gideon's of the world, we may look at our life circumstances and think maybe God has made a mistake. Maybe He could find someone else to do the job. To illustrate this point, we need only look at the alarming number of pastors who leave the ministry every month (200-1500 each *month!*) Why are so many pastors leaving the ministry? Are good pastors becoming an endangered species? Regardless of the answer to that question, I know one thing for sure, as leaders, we must stay the course!

Leadership Life Principle #2: As a leader, don't have a pity party. When the going gets tough, many of us just want to curl into a ball and give up. However, Jesus never promised us an easy life by following Him. In fact, He taught a quite different message in John 15:18 saying, "If the world hates you, keep in mind that it hated me first." Furthermore, John 16:33 says, "I have told you these things, so that in me you may have peace. In this world you will have trouble. But take heart! I have overcome the world." When the troubles of the world come your way, remember Eleazar. He stood his ground. You need to stand your ground, too.

Leadership Life Principle #3: As a leader, have your sword sharpened and ready for battle. Every soldier knows that his equipment must be in battle-ready-mode before stepping one foot on the battlefield. Have your sword sharpened and ready for battle. This takes prep time. I believe sharpening our swords occurs in our quiet times in the morning, even before the day gets started. Are you having regular, consistent, and fruitful quiet times in the morning? Are you having those times before you even crack the door open to enter the mission field? We all have a myriad of tasks we need to get accomplished within the twenty-four hours we are each given daily. We also have those things that pop up out of the blue that need attending. The problem comes when our plans clash with the things the Lord places in front of us every day—the opportunities when we can reach out to someone hurting in the spur of the moment.

Summary

In the United States there are different levels of alertness that the government has put in place called the DEFCON levels that are numbered 1 through 5. DEFCON stands for DEFense readiness CONdition. DEFCON 5 is a state of peace. DEFCON 1 typically means an active and imminent nuclear attack. As leaders, we should all be mentally prepared for DEFCON 1 as we walk out the door every day, on alert for the enemy's spiritual attacks. Ephesians 6:10-12 says:

> Finally, be strong in the Lord and in his mighty power. Put on the full armor of God so that you can take a stand against the devil's schemes. For our struggle is not against flesh and blood, but against the rulers, against the authorities, against the powers of this dark world and against the spiritual forces of evil in the heavenly realms.

CHAPTER 11
HEZEKIAH - A MAN WHO WORKED WHOLEHEARTEDLY

The Kingdom of Judah had twenty kings over the course of its history. Out of these twenty, Scripture states that twelve were evil and eight were good. This is not a particularly good track record! As you may have already guessed from this chapter's title, Hezekiah was one of the eight good kings. He was twenty-five years old when he became king of Judah, and he reigned for twenty-nine years.

Israel's line-up of kings over the years was even worse than Judah's. Out of their nineteen kings, the Bible says they *all* did evil in the eyes of the Lord.

What caused one king to choose evil, and another to choose good? Some say it was their family's heritage or their upbringing. However, we find this is not the case for Hezekiah. We don't have to look too far into 2 Kings 16 to find that King Hezekiah's father was King Ahaz, who certainly incurred a bad reputation during his reign. Who was this King Ahaz who fathered the good King Hezekiah? 2 Kings 16 describes him to us:

Unlike David his father, he did not do what was right in the eyes of the LORD his God. He walked

131

in the ways of the kings of Israel and even sacrificed his sons in the fire, following the detestable ways of the nations the LORD had driven out before the Israelites. He offered sacrifices and burned incense at the high places, on the hill tops and under every spreading tree (2 Kings 16:2-4).

King Hezekiah's only example of both a father and a king was one who did evil in the eyes of the Lord. How does a son who grows up in such a vile atmosphere turn out totally opposite of his wicked father? Here is how the Bible describes King Hezekiah:

He did what was *right in the eyes of the LORD,* just as his father David had done. He removed the high places, smashed the sacred stones and cut down the Asherah poles. He broke into pieces the bronze snake Moses had made, for up to that time the Israelites had been burning incense to it ...

Hezekiah *trusted in the LORD,* the God of Israel. There was no one like him among all of the kings of Judah, either before him or after him. *He held fast to the LORD* and did not cease to follow him; he kept the commands the LORD had given Moses. And the LORD was with him; he was successful in whatever he undertook (2 Kings 18:3-8, emphasis added).

In another passage of Scripture, the Bible describes him this way.

This is what Hezekiah did throughout Judah, *doing what was good and right and faithful before the LORD* his

God. In everything that he undertook in the service of God's temple and in obedience to the law and the commands, he *sought his God* and *worked wholeheartedly*. And so, he prospered (2 Chron 31:20-21, emphasis added).

In these verses I have highlighted several groups of words:

- Right in the eyes of the Lord
- Trusted in the Lord
- He held fast to the Lord
- Doing what was good and right and faithful before the Lord
- Sought his God and worked wholeheartedly

We could add to the back end of each of these bullet points the following: "What this means to you is—" and we would have a whole year's worth of sermons. These bullet points are the hallmarks of a faithful servant.

What can we learn from the life of King Hezekiah?

Leadership Life Principle #1: Leaders need to learn to hold fast to the Lord! We could ask ourselves, what does it mean to hold fast to the Lord? It really means putting God at the center of everything we do. It means grabbing hold of, never losing one's grip, anchoring yourself to the Lord when the trials enter our lives. Listed below are several Scriptures that attest to this principle of holding fast to the Lord.

It is the LORD your God you must follow, and him you must revere. Keep his commands and obey him; serve him and *hold fast to him* (Deut 13:4, emphasis added).

And that you may love the LORD your God, listen to his voice, and *hold fast to him*. For the LORD is your life, and he will give you many years in the land he swore to give to your fathers, Abraham, Isaac and Jacob (Deut 30:20, emphasis added).

But be very careful to keep the commandment and the law that Moses the servant of the LORD gave you: to love the LORD your God, to walk in obedience to him, to keep his commands, *to hold fast to him* and to serve him with all your heart and with all your soul (Josh 22:5, emphasis added).

Leadership Life Principle #2: Leaders need to learn how to work wholeheartedly unto the Lord. What does that mean? Merriam-Webster's online dictionary defines wholeheartedly as being "completely and sincerely devoted, determined, or enthusiastic, marked by complete earnest commitment, free from all reserve or hesitation."[6] While this definition looks good on paper, however, what does it mean in real life? What does it mean to be wholeheartedly committed as you go to work or when you volunteer in ministry?

The Bible explains the act of wholeheartedness by being replete with examples of people who worked wholeheartedly. In the next chapter we will discuss the Apostle Paul, who was a tentmaker-turned-evangelist. The Apostle Paul was sold out for the cause of Christ, and though he was only a tentmaker before, he ended up writing almost two

---

[6]*Merriam Webster,* s.v. "wholeheartedly," accessed August 12, 2020, https://www.merriam-webster.com/dictionary/wholeheartedly.

thirds of the New Testament. Paul worked relentlessly for the cause of Christ.

It is good to note here that a discussion on working wholeheartedly might fuel a workaholic's need to work even more—the workaholic being one who has made work his idol. However, remember that the body and mind both need rest. Our bodies will not function properly if it is operating at full capacity twenty-four hours a day. In fact, God instructed us to take a Sabbath rest, and set the example by resting on the seventh day after He created the world. I understand that there is a divisional line between the grace of the New Testament and the law of the Old Testament. However, there are principles of the Old Testament that should not be violated because we are New Testament Christians living under grace. So then, does the covenant of the New Testament void the Ten Commandments? I think not. Does the covenant of the New Testament void the principle of a Sabbath rest? Again, I think not.

These questions have been debated for centuries and each believer must answer them for himself. I remain firm in my belief that our bodies need down time, and over the years I have seen many exhausted, worn-out pastors and Christian leaders make horrible mistakes because of their exhaustion—sometimes even to the detriment of their families.

This is where the concept of the pendulum comes into play. If you have been with me throughout this series, you have heard me speak of the pendulum. If the pendulum swings too far to the right or the left, then your life is out of balance in some capacity. The goal of the pendulum analogy is to find the right balance in the center. When a leader finds the right balance, much can be accomplished for the Kingdom of God. When life is out of balance, families can be destroyed. Work will suffer. Ministry suffers.

I have observed pastors who've worked themselves into a health crisis, and into the hospital. I have seen others completely burn out and simply leave the ministry. Working an eighty-hour week at your career can also lead to a health crisis and burnout, leaving you with nothing left to give to your employer, to your family, or to the Lord. Conversely, I have seen pastors and lay leaders who take a lackadaisical approach to their ministry responsibilities, who neglect to do the bare minimum that their job requires. Colossians 3:22-24 gives us further perspective on how we are to work and for whom:

> Slaves, obey your earthly masters in everything; and do it, not only when their eye is on you and to win their favor, but with sincerity of heart and reverence for the Lord. *Whatever you do, work at it with all your heart, as working for the Lord, not for men,* since you know that you will receive an inheritance from the Lord as a reward. It is the Lord Christ you are serving (Col 3:22-24, emphasis added).

> God is not unjust; he will not forget *your work* and the love you have shown him as you have helped his people and continue to help them. We want each of you to show this same diligence to the very end, in order to make your hope sure. We do not want you to *become lazy,* but to imitate those who through faith and patience inherit what has been promised (Heb 6:10-12 emphasis added).

Although Paul directs his Colossians 3 passage toward slaves (employees) who were considered lazy when others were not watching, it has application for ministry as well. We should not be lazy in any of our work. Colossians 3:23, "Whatever you do, work at it with all your heart, as working for the Lord, not for men" has had a dramatic impact on my work ethic throughout the years. As co-laborers we should spur one another on with this life verse. Whether we are working to pay the bills or working to further the Kingdom, we are to give it our all because we are working for the Lord.

Leadership Life Principle #3: Understand as a leader you may need to initiate reforms. 2 Chronicles 29:3 says that King Hezekiah had only been on the throne for one month before he started making changes. He opened the doors to the temple, he brought in the Levites, he reinstituted animal sacrifices, and reinstated the celebration of Passover. When all that was done, the people went out to the surrounding towns, smashing all the idols, Asherah poles, and destroying all the high places. King Hezekiah did not hesitate to immediately start correcting wrongs. One month on the throne, at the young age of twenty-five years, he instituted sweeping reform within the nation. I am impressed such a young person could execute these monumental changes. I wonder what could happen to our country if we had leaders step up and carry out immediate reforms to turn our eyes back to the Lord God as a nation.

What reforms need to occur in your life? Maybe you have been in a position of leadership for quite some time. Maybe you and your staff have been doing something for years that now needs to change. Most people do not like change. How will you institute necessary change in your sphere of influence?

Leadership Life Principle #4: Learn to make the tough calls. In 2 Kings 18, King Hezekiah was in his fourteenth year as king, and he was facing annihilation from the Assyrian king, Sennacherib. King Hezekiah knew defeat was certain, so he sent a message to Sennacherib in verse 14, "I have done wrong. Withdraw from me, and I will pay whatever you demand of me." Verse 15-16 says, "So Hezekiah gave him all the silver that was found in the temple of the Lord and in the treasuries of the royal palace. At this time Hezekiah king of Judah stripped off the gold with which he had covered the doors and doorposts of the temple of the Lord and gave it to the king of Assyria." The decision to strip the gold off the doors of the temple was an embarrassing one. However, the alternative to that was more war and presumed annihilation. As a leader, sometimes you are faced with decisions that have no good outcomes.

The next time you are up against a decision where there can be no good outcome, pray, call your people to pray, seek the favor of the Lord, call for a fast, and determine the right course of action. Above all, never forget Leadership Life Lesson #5 below—Godly leaders must always remember that God can do the impossible.

Leadership Life Principle #5: Godly leaders must always remember that God can do the impossible. In 2 Kings Chapters 18 and 19 we observe Sennacherib's threat to attack the nation. King Hezekiah received a message from Sennacherib, who was trying to intimidate him into believing that Hezekiah's God could not withstand the Assyrian army. Consequently, Hezekiah took the letter and spread it out before the Lord in the temple, crying out to Him. Shortly after this, God sent Isaiah to tell him that He was going to fight the battle for them. 2 Kings 19:35 states the outcome of this event: "That night the angel of the Lord went out and put to death a hundred and eighty-five thousand men in the Assyrian camp. When the people got up the next morning—there were all the dead bodies! So, Sennacherib king of Assyria broke camp and withdrew. He returned to Nineveh and stayed there."

Never forget the power of God in dealing with the trials of life. We can do our best to reason and ask for advice, but if we don't listen to the Lord, disasters can occur. When we do listen, though, we can have great victories. Remember, godly leaders must always remember that God can do the impossible.

Summary

King Hezekiah knew how to work wholeheartedly and effectively for God. The question is, do you? In this pandemic, you may well have had your daily job and routine consigned to home. How effective were you in working from home in the beginning? I suspect, if you were like me, because it was all new, you didn't do so well. It took time to develop habits for you to become effective working from home with kids and dogs are underfoot.

We do not know what the next week, next month or even next year will bring. Will we be back to our corporate cubicles or will working from home be our new normal? By the way, what is the new normal and how will we need to adapt? Regardless, change is in the wind. Because of that change, as leaders in a post-COVID world, we will need to be fleet-footed in adapting to ever changing leadership requirements.

We need to take our cue from the good and righteous King Hezekiah and work wholeheartedly unto the Lord in whatever He has given us to do. Whether that is in the corporate world or the ministry world, work unto the Lord and not unto man. If you need to fine tune some job-related skills, then do it! At the beginning of this pandemic, the Lord gave me three words, "Redeem the Time." Beloved, redeem the time

CHAPTER 12

PAUL - A MAN WHO GAVE IT HIS ALL

It is fitting that we end this series with the great Apostle Paul, a man who gave it his all. In his early years, Paul had been a well-trained Pharisee who had studied under Gamaliel, one of the finest teachers of the day. I suspect that Paul's education would be akin to one receiving a doctorate from Harvard University today. Furthermore, Paul was extremely religious and he spent most of his life as a Pharisee, meaning he was well-versed in Hebrew and the Jewish traditions. Being Jewish also meant that Paul most likely began learning spiritual things when he was around five years old, and then starting formal training at the age of ten.

With the exception of Jesus Christ, Paul—under the divine inspiration of the Holy Spirit—helped shape Christian doctrine more than anyone else in Scripture.

We first meet Paul (called Saul at that time) in Acts 8:1, as he oversees and approves the stoning of Stephen. Saul was clearly a fierce defender of the Jewish tradition. This personality trait of Saul's has led some to believe that since he was alive during Jesus's earthly ministry, Saul might have been in Jerusalem when Christ was taken to the cross. I suspect that Saul also understood that the new sect—The Way, which was soon to become the Christian faith—was a significant threat to the Jewish tradition. Therefore, Saul went on a vicious and fanatical campaign to eradicate this new religious movement. In Acts 8:3 we read, "But Saul began to destroy the church. Going house to house, he dragged off men and women and put them in prison." However, the good news was not to be tamed. Verse 4 says, "Those who had been scattered preached the word wherever they went."

This is the unique and incomprehensible trait of the Christian faith. Time after time has proven that when the Christian faith has been persecuted, it explodes even further and faster, winning new converts to the knowledge of the saving grace of Jesus Christ. This faith was unlike other faiths which Saul had undoubtedly confronted in his line of work.

Acts 9:1 reads, "Meanwhile, Saul was still *breathing out murderous threats* against the Lord's disciples. He went to the high priest and asked him for letters to the synagogues in Damascus, so that if he found any there who belonged to the Way, whether men or women, he might take them as prisoners to Jerusalem" (emphasis added). Saul's breathing out murderous threats conjures up an evil and destructive image of a terrorist. I imagine Saul was violently fanatical in his cause, much like a leader of the modern-day terrorist groups Boko Haram or Al Qaeda.

Notice Saul asked permission of the high priest to further his campaign and continue his reign of terror in Damascus. It was on this road to Damascus that Saul had a power-encounter with Jesus. A bright light surrounded him, and he heard a heavenly voice surround him. Saul fell to the ground, hearing, but not seeing. In that moment, Saul's life was forever changed. This story has led me to tell inmates—and anyone else who would listen—that you cannot have a power-encounter with Jesus and walk away unchanged. Saul met the living Savior of the world, face-to-face. Unsurprisingly, when Saul got up from the ground, he was blind. He went to Judas's house on Straight Street, and there he remained blind for three days.

Have you ever thought about what Paul might have been thinking while he was at Judas's house? Can you even imagine what you would be thinking if, in an instant, everything you thought was sacred in your life turned out to be wrong? Think about the passion Paul had in persecuting the church, and how he now knew he had been profoundly wrong. Think about how you would've reacted! Think about the ramifications your belief structure would sustain if you had been Saul, and had finally realized that Jesus really was who He said He was. Paul later states in Galatians 1:11-18,

> I want you to know, brothers, that the gospel I preached is not something that man made up. I did not receive it from any man, nor was I taught it, rather, I received it by revelation from Jesus Christ. For you have heard of my previous way of life in Judaism, how intensely I persecute the church of God and tried to destroy it. I was advancing in Judaism beyond many Jews of my own age and was extremely jealous for the traditions of my fathers. But when God, who set me apart from birth and called me by his grace was pleased to reveal his Son in me so that I might preach him among the Gentiles, *I did not consult any man, nor did I go up to Jerusalem* to see those who were apostles before I was, but I went immediately into Arabia and later returned to Damascus. Then after *three years*, I went up to Jerusalem to get acquainted with Peter and stayed with him fifteen days (emphasis added).

Many people question why Paul went to Arabia and why he stayed there for three years. Some scholars believe that he went to Arabia because there were no Apostles in Arabia to give him personal instruction as declared in verses 11 and 12. Some speculate the three years he spent in Arabia was similar to the three years that the original Apostles spent with Jesus during His ministry.

Either way, I believe these three years were used in preparation for what lay ahead for Paul. Though the Bible is silent on this matter, some further speculate that Paul was taught the ways of Jesus either by Christ himself or by the Holy Spirit. Regardless of how he learned what he learned, it was in these years that Paul realized his purpose in life, which was to preach to the Gentiles.

Understandably, Paul found himself under immense suspicion from the Jews as well from the Christians after his conversion. Neither side trusted him. Once he was finally accepted by the Christians, the Jews detested him. They made Paul suffer tremendously, causing him to lose everything—his position within the community, his status as a Pharisee, and many of his friends. As believers in Christ, we should be indebted to him for what he had to endure so that we, the pagan Gentiles, could hear the message of salvation and be grafted into the Vine.

It is worthwhile to note the lengths that God goes to get our attention. Prior to his Damascus road experience, Saul had been a strict Pharisee. As God sometimes does, He used a spiritual "two-by-four" to get Saul's attention. It is not unusual for God to do this for us. In fact, I have been on the other end of that spiritual "two-by-four" twice in my life. The first time when I was on the cusp of losing my wife and unborn child to preeclampsia during childbirth in 1981. The other time was when the stock market crashed on October 19, 1987. The first jolt was to save my soul. The latter jolt was to set my life on a course to preach the good news to the inmates of the world.

Life and ministry can be inexplicably difficult at times for me, fraught with many differing personality styles and stretching moments. There are always funding issues and the constant concern that I have for the inmate churches around the world. When ministry becomes difficult, I always go back to 2 Corinthians 11:23-28, which contains a list of life experiences the great Apostle Paul endured as he was preaching the Good News. This passage is the anecdote for any pity party I might be tempted to throw for myself. When I am done reading this text, I shake my head in disgust at being bound up with anger, frustration, or anxiety. Read this list of what I call Paul's ministry stripes:

> I have worked much harder, been in prison more frequently, been flogged more severely, and been exposed to death again and again. Five times I received from the Jews the forty lashes minus one. Three times I was beaten with rods, once I was stoned, three times I was shipwrecked, I spent a night and a day in the open sea, I have been constantly on the move. I have been in danger from rivers, in danger from bandits, in danger from my own countrymen, in danger from Gentiles; in danger in the city, in danger in the country, in danger at sea; and in danger from false brothers. I have labored and toiled and have often gone without sleep; I have known hunger and thirst and have often gone without food; I have been cold and naked. Besides everything else, I face daily the pressure of my concern for all the churches (2 Cor 11:23-28).

This is what this man suffered so that you and I could know the saving grace of Jesus Christ. Paul was a man who gave it his all. As I mentioned earlier, I believe those three years Paul spent in Arabia were in preparation for a lifetime of struggles he would face as he fulfilled his calling to minister to the Gentiles.

Thus far in life, the struggles I have experienced in life, pale in comparison to what Paul endured. Two thousand years later, I am living an abundant life in Christ because of what Paul and all those saints who went before me had endured. I am eternally grateful for their sacrifices. I hope, if the Lord tarries, many inmates around the world will have that same freedom in Christ, brought to them by ordinary men and women of faith.

I'd be remiss not to mention in today's America, we have this dysfunctional thinking that if a life, ministry, or church is not prospering, then there must be something wrong with it. There must be sin in the camp. However, we need only read 2 Corinthians 11:23-29—where Paul lists his many struggles in ministry—to understand this thought is far from accurate. We can also look at the life of Job when his friends questioned him on what he did to anger God. These passages show that this cancerous thinking is not from God, but rather from ones living in a prosperous society. It is ingrained in us from the moment we start school that those who excel are rewarded. Also, as in the case of Shadrach, Meshach, and Abednego, we see that they were cast into a blazing furnace because of the will of God being worked in their lives, not something they had brought on themselves.

Like all those I've mentioned above, Paul also persevered. He ran the race marked out for him. He didn't quit. He didn't retire. Paul was a man who gave it his all.

What can we learn from the life of Paul?

Leadership Life Principle #1: Understand no one is outside of God's reach. Those who share the Gospel on a regular basis knows this statement to be fact. Others who do not share the Gospel on a regular basis may not understand how this can be possible. Over the last thirty-five years of prison ministry I have found this statement to be conclusively true. Some of those with the hardest of hearts have bowed their knee to Jesus and are serving Him in fulltime ministry today. We have a saying at PFC whenever we hear of a life transforming testimony: "This is why we do what we do!"

Paul used to shout out murderous threats, dragging Christians from their homes, and throwing them into prison. If he could get saved, *anyone* can get saved. I have heard stories from around the world of people, even those involved in terrorism, getting saved. So what would you say if an anarchist of the Antifa flavor—decked out in their black garb—came to you and told you he or she had just received Christ? What would you think in the recesses of your mind? I can only imagine what the disciples must have thought when Paul came to them. The Bible says that Paul went and stayed with Peter for fifteen days. Oh, how I would have loved to have sat in on that conversation. Can you imagine Paul's excitement? Can you imagine Peter's skepticism? What would you do it he had come to you? Or, to put it in today's thinking, what if that former Antifa came to you and asked you for help? What would you say?

As a leader, don't prejudge someone by his looks or demeanor. Don't think to yourself that this poor soul is beyond the reach of God. Praise God for this new creation in Christ and start taking those first baby steps of discipleship. Remember, when it comes time for new believers to start serving in the body of Christ, do not discard them. They have a lot to offer believers of all maturity levels.

Leadership Life Principle #2: Recognize our past blunders, mistakes, and sinful lifestyle choices do not define us. Paul is an excellent example of this Leadership Life Principle. The Bible is rife with examples of those who—based on outwards appearances—should be disqualified from being used by God. Many preachers today are behind the pulpit because they found Jesus inside a prison cell, or in the emergency room after overdosing on opioids, or even in the dinner hall of the city mission. Many missionaries in the field today, on the other side of the world, came from similar backgrounds. These men and women are great warriors for the cause of Christ.

The interesting thing about souls with a checkered past is that their previous lifestyles often had them putting all their time and energy into their destructive choices. When they come to Christ they typically don't slow their energy levels down—they just redirect their drives into Kingdom business. This is fantastic news for the church and many parachurch organizations.

Though mature believers may want them to slow down (as in stop talking about Jesus all the time!), these new Christians often can't. They know what Jesus has saved them from, and they want everyone else to know what they know, now! This is a beautiful thing. Don't try to put a muzzle or put a leash on them—let them run. Their style and methodology may grate on you, but they are children of the King, called to be used for His purposes. Nurture them. Guide them. Instruct them.

Leadership Life Principle #3: Realize that sometimes we need to lose our sight, to see. Who would ever imagine losing one's eyesight to be a good thing? This is exactly what happened to Paul after his road to Damascus conversion experience. For three days he was blind. As I mentioned before, this loss of sight is the spiritual two-by-four that God used to get his attention. In Acts 9, we learn that the Lord sent Ananias to the house of Judas on Straight Street. Ananias prayed for Paul, and immediately something like scales dropped off his eyes.

Once he regained his sight, Paul immediately took action. The Bible reports in Acts 9:18-21:

> Immediately, something like scales fell from Saul's eyes and he could see again. *He got up and was baptized*, and after taking some food, he regained his strength. Saul spent several days with the disciples in Damascus. *At once he began to preach* in the synagogue that Jesus is the son of God. All those who heard him were astonished (emphasis added).

What an incredible testimony. Only after several days did he start preaching. He didn't spend years in seminary. After some training from the disciples in Damascus, he immediately started preaching.

As leaders, we need to be men and women of action. Don't wait. People are dying every day and entering a Christ-less eternity. In the season of time we are living, this is especially important. Time is of the essence. Don't hesitate. Don't withdraw. Be like Paul, a man who gave it his all!

Summary

This concludes the last lesson of *Biblical Leadership in Turbulent Times- Book Two- Lessons Learned from Good Biblical Leaders*. To gain the most out of this book, it is important to evaluate yourself on these twelve chapters' principles. Once complete, further drill down to evaluate yourself on each of the sixty Leadership Life Principles.

In the appendix, you will find a Bible study for each chapter. Each lesson has ten to fifteen self-reflective questions to assist you in growing your leadership for each chapters' principles. You may choose to do a self-study— this is always a good place to start. However, I would recommend you gather several like-minded men or women with varying degrees of leadership levels. Work through each lesson together. As a quick start, you could meet to study one lesson each week. That track would take you three months to complete the block of lessons. With bi-monthly lesson meeting times, every other week, it would take six months to complete the lessons. Likewise, a once-a-month meeting schedule would take a year to complete. There are pros and cons to each meeting frequency. The quick start allows you to get through the entire block of lessons quicker, but does not give you much time to work on issues in between lessons.

I would encourage you to list five to ten leaders whom you could invite to your Bible study. Propose to them that you do a rotational teaching schedule, giving everyone a session to teach, allowing for the spreading of the workload.

APPENDIX

EXHIBIT A
SELF-REFLECTION EXERCISE

Take a moment to complete this self-examination review on chapter three. On the left-hand side of each number assign a value between one and ten, ten being the highest, as how you see your proficiencies in each of the Leadership Life Principles (LLP's) as listed in each of the chapters. Be honest. In the last self-evaluation review in *Basic Principles for Christians Leaders* you were instructed to give this test to your spouse to help identify areas of similarities and areas which might have large deltas–differentials. However, in this self-evaluation, your spouse or your staff may not know you well enough to give you constructive criticism in each of the LLPs. Mark n/a for any areas that may not pertain to you.

1. People of vision are moved to action by some external input.
2. People of vision fast and pray before deciding on the course of action.
3. People of vision count the costs before starting any major project.
4. People of vision understand they need to make presentations to those who can aid them in their quest such as donors, stakeholders, bosses, superiors, or politicians.
5. People of vision assess the current situation surrounding a project.

6. People of vision recruit a team to assist in executing a project.
7. People of vision train and instruct their team.
8. People of vision fight the battles that arise during their ventures.
9. People of vision execute the vision God has given to them.
10. People of vision manage to keep the team motivated during the mission.
11. People of vision complete the task at hand.
12. People of vision praise the Lord upon completion.

Instructions:

1. If you rate yourself in any one item less than 7 you need to take immediate action to identify how to correct the problem.
2. If you have rated yourself less than 5 in any one area, you need immediate help in changing course.

EXHIBIT B
CORRECTIVE ACTION

1. Using the list in Exhibit B, list all attributes that you rated yourself less than 7.
2. Write out a problem statement for each. What do you see are the symptoms of the problem? What pain do you experience from this problem? What needs to change for this problem to be corrected?
3. List three possible action items you can take to correct this weakness.

Attribute number and name:

Problem Statement: Allow the Holy Spirit to reveal you why you are weak in this area. List this in the form of a problem statement.

Corrective action: What three things can you do to correct this leadership deficiency?

1.

2.

3.

EXHIBIT C
SIXTY LEADERSHIP LIFE PRINCIPLES FOR REVIEW

There are twelve chapters in this book with sixty Leadership Life Principles. It would be easy to complete this reading and forget some of the key issues that the Lord used to speak to your heart. Use this appendix to review the LLPs that spoke to your heart, making notes or rating yourself in each area.

Chapter 1 – Joseph - A Man of Administration

Leadership Life Principle #1: Always seek God's favor in your life.

Leadership Life Principle #2: Learn to be proven faithful in the little things of life.

Leadership Life Principle #3: Endeavor to grow in your administrative giftedness.

Leadership Life Principle #4: Learn to stay organized.

Chapter 2 – Moses - A Man of Delegation

Leadership Life Principle #1: Learn to listen to God.

Leadership Life Principle #2: Commit to being teachable.

Leadership Life Principle #3: Learn to lead many.

Leadership Life Principle #4: Learn to be humble at all times.

Leadership Life Principle #5: Allow God to fight your battles for you.

Leadership Life Principle #6: Implement the art of delegating.

Chapter 3 – Nehemiah - A Man of Great Vision

Leadership Life Principle #1: People of vision are moved to action by some external input.

Leadership Life Principle #2: People of vision fast and pray before deciding on the course of action.

Leadership Life Principle #3: People of vision count the costs before starting any major project.

Leadership Life Principle #4: People of vision understand they need to make presentations to those who can aid them in their quest such as donors, stakeholders, bosses, superiors, or politicians.

Leadership Life Principle #5: People of vision assess the current situation surrounding a project.

Leadership Life Principle #6: People of vision recruit a team to assist in executing a project.

Leadership Life Principle #7: People of vision train and instruct their team.

Leadership Life Principle #8: People of vision fight the battles that arise during their ventures.

Leadership Life Principle #9: People of vision execute the vision God has given to them.

Leadership Life Principle #10: People of vision manage to keep the team motivated during the mission.

Leadership Life Principle #11: People of vision complete the task at hand.

Leadership Life Principle #12: People of vision praise the Lord upon completion.

Chapter 4 – Daniel - A Man Above Reproach

Leadership Life Principle #1: Live your life according to God's standards.

Leadership Life Principle #2: Live your life above reproach.

Leadership Life Principle #3: When you work, work above reproach.

Leadership Life Principle #4: When you make a mistake, admit to it quickly.

Leadership Life Principle #5: Do not throw in your hat with evil doers.

Chapter 5 – Shadrach, Meshach, and Abednego - Men Secure in their Convictions

Leadership Life Principle #1: Understand that the trials of life are not necessarily an indication of God's withdrawal or His punishment.

Leadership Life Principle #2: Instead of pleading with God to extricate you from the fiery furnace of trials, discover Jesus in the fire.

Leadership Life Principle #3: We will never lead a dying world to Christ by blending in with the mainstream culture.

Leadership Life Principle #4: Understand that if God answered all our prayers the way we want, there would be no reason for faith.

Leadership Life Principle #5: Realize that to be a leader who understands conviction, you need to get out on the limb and be counted.

Leadership Life Principle #6: In the end times, expect the furnace to be heated up seventy-times-seven hotter.

Chapter 6 – Caleb - A Man of Courage

Leadership Life Principle #1: As a leader, dwell in the land of promises, not in the land of giants.

Leadership Life Principle #2: Understand words are extremely powerful—whether they are used for the positive or the negative reasoning.

Leadership Life Principle #3: Don't allow yourself to be contaminated with stinking thinking.

Leadership Life Principle #4: Realize some leaders remain resilient way beyond their years.

Leadership Life Principle #5: Resolve to speak when the Holy Spirit prompts you to speak!

Leadership Life Principle #6: Commit to being a man or woman of courage.

Chapter 7 – Gideon - A Man Who Listened to the Voice of God

Leadership Life Principle #1: Understand that God can use you despite your limitations.

Leadership Life Principle #2: Realize man looks at the outward appearance, but God looks at the heart.

Leadership Life Principle #3: God desires to help His servants increase their faith.

Leadership Life Principle #4: When God asks you to do something, don't make excuses.

Chapter 8 – Jonathan - A Man of Loyalty

Leadership Life Principle #1: Understand we were created to be in relationship with God first and others second.

Leadership Life Principle #2: Understand loyalty is a two-way street.

Leadership Life Principle #3: Understand to be in a loyal relationship both parties must be transparent.

Chapter 9 – David - A Man of Strategic Planning

Leadership Life Principle #1: Purpose to become a strategic thinker.

Leadership Life Principle #2: Learn to inquire of the Lord about any new idea or direction.

Leadership Life Principle #3: Realize to be a leader today requires courage.

Chapter 10 – Eleazar - A Man Who Would Not Retreat

Leadership Life Principle #1: As a leader, stay the course when the going gets tough.

Leadership Life Principle #2: As a leader, don't have a pity party.

Leadership Life Principle #3: As a leader, have your sword sharpened and ready for battle.

Chapter 11 – Hezekiah - A Man Who Worked Wholeheartedly

Leadership Life Principle #1: Leaders need to learn to hold fast to the Lord!

Leadership Life Principle #2: Leaders need to learn how to work wholeheartedly unto the Lord.

Leadership Life Principle #3: Understand as a leader you may need to initiate reforms.

Leadership Life Principle #4: Learn to make the tough calls.

Leadership Life Principle #5: Godly leaders must always remember that God can do the impossible.

Chapter 12 – Paul - A Man Who Gave It His All

Leadership Life Principle #1: Understand no one is outside of God's reach.

Leadership Life Principle #2: Recognize our past blunders, mistakes, and sinful lifestyle choices do not define us.

Leadership Life Principle #3: Realize that sometimes we need to lose our sight, to see.

ABOUT PRISONERS FOR CHRIST
OUTREACH MINISTRIES

Let me take a few more minutes of your time and tell you a little more about Prisoners For Christ Outreach Ministries (PFC). PFC is a ministry dedicated to taking the Gospel of Jesus Christ to the institutions of the world. As of the close of 2019, we had over 1,500 volunteers worldwide and we are growing every day. Last year, our volunteers conducted an average of 510 church services per month, more than 16 services per day. PFC had a yearly attendance count of over 967,000 at our services last year, with over 66,700 men, women, and children accepting Jesus Christ as Lord and Savior for the first time.

Originally started in the state of Washington, PFC has field offices in eighteen different countries, including Burkina Faso, Burundi, Cameroon, Congo-DRC, Ethiopia, India, Kenya, Malawi, Nepal, Niger, Nigeria, Russia, Rwanda, Sierra Leonne, Tanzania, the Philippines, Togo, and Uganda, with more than ten other countries waiting to be accepted.

In addition, PFC has a two-year Bible study correspondence course and a pen-pal program, as well as our national inmate newspaper, *Yard Out*, for inmates here in the United States. We exist for the sole purpose of sharing the love of Christ to the lost in the prisons of the world.

Our major objective is to win souls to Christ. Our secondary objective is to equip the saints to do good works while in the sphere of prison ministry. Whether you are an individual prison volunteer going into one institution, or whether you are a part of a larger team, or even perhaps a volunteer in your church's prison outreach, we are interested in you! We are interested in your development as a minister of the Gospel. So please avail yourself of our training and the printed resources found on our web page, www.prisonersforchrist.org.

If the Lord should ever tug on your heart to be a part of the PFC team worldwide, we have several opportunities of involvement for you.

1. If you have a loved one in prison and desire some Christian literature be sent to that person, please go online at www.prisonersforchrist.org to submit a literature request.

2. If you would like to receive our current annual report or register for our newsletter, either in print or electronically, please go to the website to request copies.

3. If you would like to volunteer or develop a PFC outpost in your state, please go to the website and ask for our franchise brochure. See more on the franchise ministry in the subsequent pages.

4. If you were blessed by this book, you can donate either by mailing a check to our PFC offices or by giving online through our web page. Please go to the same site and at the bottom of the page and click "Give."

Whether you are here in the United States or living in another part of the world, please consider joining the family of PFC. However, if you are a part of another existing prison ministry, stay where you are and be the best prison ministry volunteer for that organization. In other words, "Bloom where you are planted!"

Feel free to connect with us in one of several ways:

1. Mailing address:
   Prisoners For Christ (PFC)
   PO Box 1530
   Woodinville, WA 98072
2. Web page: www.prisonersforchrist.org
3. PFC Facebook: https://www.facebook.com/Prisoners-for-Christ-Outreach-Ministries-76125072756
4. Office phone: (425) 483-4151
5. Author's Personal Facebook: www.facebook.com/gregvontobel
6. Author's LinkedIn: www.linkedin.com/in/greg-von-tobel-67832548/
7. Author's Twitter: www.twitter.com/GregVonTobel
8. Author's Instagram: www.instagram.com/gregvontobel/

SMALL GROUP BIBLE STUDIES

WEEK 1
JOSEPH - A MAN OF ADMINISTRATION

1. Read Genesis 39:1-6. Once Joseph was sold to Potiphar, we learn more about Potiphar and his household. The fact the Bible describes Potiphar as one of Pharaoh's officials and the captain of the guard, eludes to his standing in Egypt. Potiphar, in all probability, was appointed by the Pharaoh, making him a very wealthy man who had a prominent position within the country and an audience with Pharaoh. Potiphar was over the prisons in the land. Do you think Potiphar was organized in his business and household dealings or do you think he was highly unorganized? Please explain your answer to the group.

2. Read Genesis 39:20-23. Here we have the second example of Joseph being elevated to a different tier of leadership for two reasons. First, God's favor on his life. Second, because of Joseph's giftedness in the areas of administration and management. Always remember this statement: "Where God calls, God equips." What do verses 22-23 tell you about the warden and how he felt about Joseph? Do you think this happened overnight or do you think Joseph had to prove himself? Read Luke 16:10. How does this verse in Luke play into your answer?

3. Read Genesis 41:39-41, 44, 46. This is the third and last level of leadership promotions God gives to Joseph. In

the first example, Joseph oversaw an official's household. In the second example, he oversaw an entire prison. In this third example, he oversaw an entire country. How old was Joseph when the Pharaoh promoted him (vs. 46)? What is the enormity of this third promotion?

4. Read Exodus 32:11, Nehemiah 1:11. In these examples we can observe that the Lord was with both Moses and Nehemiah shining His favor upon them. In this chapter we are apt to conclude that the Lord shone His favor on Joseph's life as well. Is it wrong to pray for God's favor or success in your life? Have you ever prayed for favor from God? Please explain to the group.

5. How would you rate yourself as being organized in your work life? How about your home life? Is there a difference between your ability of being more organized in your work life versus your home life or vice versa? Please explain to the group why this might be.

6. What obstacles do you have to overcome for you to get to the next level of organization?

7. I suspect, in question 6, one answer for many is that you have too many messes in your life or you're over-committed in too many areas. Let's start with a mess in your life. What is a mess? A mess is anything that is a distraction that takes your mind and energy away from

what you should be doing. These messes could be your fault, or they may be messes brought on by others. It doesn't matter how it got to be a mess, but a mess is a mess. Messes distract us from what we are called to do. First, list all the messes you have at work. Then list all the messes you have at home. How many messes did you list from work? From home? If you feel comfortable with the group, share several of those messes and what caused them.

8. The longer it takes to overcome a mess is directly proportional to the level of complexity of said mess. For example, a messy garage may take a day or two to clean up. Rehabbing a bathroom can take a month. Dealing with a tax audit can take significantly longer. Dealing with legal issues or litigation are monsters that take up enormous amounts of time. How much time will it take to clean up all your messes - one week, one month, six months, one year? Can you delegate any of these messes to others?

9. What will cleaning up your messes enable you to do? Will this free up your mental agility?

10. Let's deal with the second part of question 7, being overcommitted. Are you overcommitted? Ask your spouse if he or she thinks you are overcommitted. You will get the real answer. How did you get to this point? The simple answer is that, for whatever reason, you couldn't say no to someone. Busy people get more done than non-busy people. The age-old adage is true,

"If you want something done, give it to a busy person." The more complicated answer is that you did not evaluate your time and current priorities. If you are over-committed and have multiple messes in your life, you have the perfect storm. You most likely have stress swirling around your life. Review your extracurricular commitment level once again. Determine if you can keep going as is or if you need to cut back. Share with the group. Do you need to take a sabbatical, not from your job, but from all your extracurricular activities? In the last thirty-five years of ministry I have taken three sabbaticals of this type. I either permanently resigned or temporarily resigned from all extracurricular activities, committee meetings, Board member meetings, and volunteer work. Do you need to take a sabbatical?

11. Once you have cleaned up your messes and reviewed your commitment level, you can focus on becoming more organized. What can you do to get to the next level of efficiency to stay more organized? You will have to look through a new set of lenses to review the processes you go through daily. How organized are you with physical paperwork or digital paperwork? What can you do differently to remain more focused? Share with your group your ideas.

12. Is there any new technology that you can incorporate into your workday?

13. What three things did the Holy Spirit reveal to you about this lesson on the life of Joseph?

A.

B.

C.

14. Make a list of five items that need to happen to help you become more organized.

A.

B.

C.

D.

E.

WEEK 2
MOSES - A MAN OF DELEGATION

1. Read Exodus 18:23. What was Moses doing in verse 13? How many people were potentially in the camp he was overseeing? Read Exodus 12:37.

2. Read Exodus 18:14-16. Jethro, Moses' father-in-law, observes his son-in-law and asks Moses two questions in Exodus 18:14. Moses responded to his two questions in verse 15 and 16. What were the two reasons Moses gave in response to his father-in-law's questions?

3. Jethro makes a pretty bold statement in verse 17. What were the consequences if Moses did not accept his advice as described in verse18? Have you ever received advice from your father-in-law? How did you react? Did you take his advice well, or did you toss it out the window? Why?

4. Read verses 20-23. Jethro gave Moses six pieces of advice. List them. Which ones spoke to your heart?

5. In verse 21, Jethro gave Moses criteria for selecting capable men. What three things did Jethro advise in selecting capable leaders? Is that good business advice for today or was that only good for back then? How

can we apply that to our business or ministry lives to-day?

6. What is the natural outcome of implementing this strategy as listed in verses 22 and 23?

7. Do you believe yourself to be a good delegator? Explain your answer to your group. If no, what are your problem areas?

8. Are you afraid to delegate? Why? Have you ever had a bad experience when delegating? Did that experience cost you anything? How well did you respond when you saw it going sideways? How could you have corrected the problem before it got to be a problem? Speak freely with your group without naming names.

9. Have you ever thought this? "If you want a job done right, then do it yourself." Why does that statement create a catastrophic mindset in learning to delegate? What must you do to break out of that mindset?

10. In chapter two of this book, I list seven reasons why people fail to delegate. Name your two most problematic areas from this list of seven. Why are these areas a problem for you? List how you can correct these problems.

11. I also listed seven ways you can overcome these obstacles. Which two areas that will help you the most in overcoming these obstacles? Explain to the group which ones you chose.

12. Do you believe you should be delegating more?

13. What do you need to do to become proficient in delegating?

14. What three things did the Holy Spirit reveal to you to about this lesson on delegation and the life of Moses?

    A.

    B.

    C.

15. Make a list of five items that need to occur to help you in becoming more proficient in delegating.

    A.

    B.

    C.

    D.

    E.

WEEK 3
NEHEMIAH - A MAN OF GREAT VISION

1. Read Nehemiah 1:1-11. A visionary is anyone who sees a need and sets out to solve that need. Expected traits of visionaries are that they are super intelligent, to be very charismatic, and to have many other intellectual abilities. We might think of Bill Gates of Microsoft, Elon Musk of Tesla, or Jeff Bezos of Amazon in this category. Yes, these men are visionaries. However, using them as a benchmark gives a distorted picture of being a visionary. I have seen children in the news who saw a need and set a course to solve the problem. You can be a manager overseeing only one employee and still be a visionary. You can be a housewife overseeing a home and still be a visionary. What do you believe are the traits of being a visionary? Do you have those traits? What do you need to do to enhance and grow some of those traits?

2. In America we have the saying, "Build a better mouse trap." That means whatever you are doing find a better, more efficient way to do or to produce things. When we think of visionaries we think of for-profit entities. Visionaries can also be in the nonprofit sector or be involved in church related activities. You can be a youth pastor or a senior pastor. You can be a mom or an inmate in the prison church. Do you see yourself as a visionary? Why or why not?

3. What was the bad news Nehemiah heard in Nehemiah 1:3? Why did this news trouble Nehemiah?

4. What were the three things Nehemiah did immediately after hearing the news? What was the order in which he did them? Do you understand the power of fasting? Do you fast on a regular basis?[7]

5. Read Nehemiah 2:1-9. Nehemiah knew he could not accomplish the building of the wall alone. He needed manpower and financial resources. Leadership Life Principle #4 in this chapter states, "People of vision understand they need to make presentations to those who can aid them in their quest such as donors, stake-holders, bosses, superiors, or politicians." Do you believe this is a true statement? Why or why not? Does this part of being a visionary scare you? Please explain your answer to the group. In Nehemiah 2:2 the Bible reads, "I was very much afraid," Why was Nehemiah afraid?

6. Read Nehemiah 2:11-18. Leadership Life Principle #5 says "People of vision assess the current state of affairs surrounding a project." Read Luke 14:28-30. Why is it so important to count the costs before embarking on a project? Have you ever found yourself in the middle of a project and realized it was going to cost way more than you had anticipated? What went wrong? How did

---

[7] I believe all great works of God should be preceded with a season of fasting. Fasting is a very misunderstood spiritual discipline, some believe is used only by the religious fanatics of today. If you want to know more about fasting pick up my book *Staving Off Disaster- A Journey in Spiritual Fasting, A Guide for Christians in Times of Crisis* at Amazon.

you underestimate the costs? Did you build in any buffers?

7. In Nehemiah 3:1-32 is the assignment of the work of rebuilding the wall. In Chapter 2 of this book, we talked about Moses, who learned how to delegate. In Nehemiah, we see the same thing happen. Nehemiah was delegating and assigning tasks. Visionaries can get a bad rap. They are sometimes criticized for being too scattered and not communicating properly. Why is it so important to set the course, to stay on that course, and to give clear instruction? How do you measure up in these areas?

8. In any great undertaking there are going to be defining moments where one comes to a crossroad of deciding whether to go forward, take another direction, or retreat altogether. If you are leading the team, you bear much of that stress. This is where morale of the team can be at an all-time low. As a visionary, what can you do to elevate morale and keep the momentum going?

9. In chapter 3 in Leadership Life Lessons #8, there are six different obstacles Nehemiah had to overcome. I don't suspect many of us have ever experienced all six of these issues when working on a project. List those areas that you have experienced while working on a project. How did that make you feel? These obstacles were only distractions used by the enemy to slow or stop the work of God. Why is it so important to identify these distractions as the work of the enemy? Explain to the group how you have overcome these frustration and morale slumps.

10. Review the twelve Leadership Life Lessons listed in chapter 3. List the two areas you struggle the most with and why.

11. List two areas in which you excel. Try to determine the difference between those you listed as struggles and those where you excel.

12. What three things did the Holy Spirit reveal to you about this lesson on being a visionary?

A.

B.

C.

13. Make a list of five tasks that need to occur to help you become more proficient in becoming a visionary.

A.

B.

C.

D.

E.

WEEK 4
DANIEL - A MAN ABOVE REPROACH

1. Read Daniel 6:1-3. Human nature has not changed. People get envious. They get jealous. The same thing that Daniel experienced in 537 BC is still occurring twenty-five hundred years later, across the world in corporations, churches, and non-profits today. Have you ever been in a position where you were promoted for a job well done only to discover you had those who were envious of your promotion? Did they try to sabotage your future work? Did they cause division within the organization?

2. Read Daniel 6:4. The Bible says, "They could find no corruption in him, because he was trustworthy and neither corrupt not negligent." Scholars believe Daniel was eighty years old when this biblical event occurred. He had been around the proverbial block, meaning he had some work history that people could examine to see if he was corrupt or negligent. In verse 4 it lists three attributes of Daniel. What were those three attributes? How do you measure up in these areas?

3. It is only natural that nefarious individuals with wrong motives, who seek to tear you down, who can't find anything in your background that would cause people to question your work ethics, will attempt to go after your belief structure. If you are a leader in a secular organization, you will experience this much more so than

someone who works in a Christian workplace. Have you ever had someone at work try to bait you into a conversation so you would publicly take a stance on social issues that are aligned to the Word of God? How did you respond? What was the outcome?

4. Read Daniel 6:6-10. Daniel, according to his convictions, determined he had to take a stand. What was that stand? The world is in chaos and spinning out of control. Absent spiritual revival there is no hope. Persecution is on its way. How are you preparing spiritually and physically for this coming persecution?

5. Daniel was a man who lived his life above reproach. What does it mean to live your life above reproach? Have you ever been asked to not be forthright in any business communication? Have you ever been asked to falsify reports or stats? Have you ever been asked to skew data? Has a workplace friend ever asked you do to something that wasn't right? Compromise is easy. Standing up to wrongful requests is not. The past is the past. The past does not define your future. How are you going to respond to those requests in the future?

6. Having a clear conscience is the best antidote for wrongful requests. Live your life above reproach. If you make a mistake own up to it, quickly. Why is it so important to own up to your mistakes quickly? What were the consequences of not owning up to one of your mistakes in the past?

7. Never allow anyone to have leverage over you for some of your past decisions. This only perpetuates incessant manipulation. Read Ecclesiastes 12:13. How does this Scripture bring this more to light?

8. Read Colossians 3:23. How does this Scripture put things into perspective? Define what the first part of this Scripture means, "Whatever you do, work at it with all of your heart."

9. What does the latter part of Colossians 3:23 "as working for the Lord, not for men" mean?

10. As a leader, you need to protect your good name and your reputation. That is why this lesson on living your life above reproach is so vitally important. What can you do to change personal habits that, if known, might call your reputation into question?

11. Daniel decided to honor God rather than be disobedient. He understood the costs—life or death. Christians around the world are facing those same decisions every day. What can you do today in fighting compromise that might help you when more drastic persecution stands at your door and knocks?

12. What three things did the Holy Spirit reveal to you about this lesson on living your life above reproach?

A.

B.

C.

13. Make a list of five items that will help you in becoming more proficient in living your life above reproach.

A.

B.

C.

D.

E.

WEEK 5

SHADRACH, MESHACH, AND ABEDNEGO - MEN SECURE IN THEIR CONVICTIONS

1. Read Daniel 3:1-18. Here we have a story of three young men who were exported from their homeland to a foreign land. These three young men were friends. What is your definition of a friend? You should have loyalty in your definition as explained in Chapter 2, the kind experienced through the life of David and Jonathan. Do you have close friends who you can count on? Please explain.

2. It is much easier to go through a trial with close friends than to go through a trial without any friends. Women have a much easier time in making friends then men do. Think of the last trial that you walked through. Did you have friends walking through that trial with you? Were they checking in on you regularly? Were you disappointed with any of their responses? How would you vocalize your disappointment if asked?

3. These three men in Daniel 3—Shadrach, Meshach, and Abednego—were close friends that were confronted by the king after refusing to bow down to the king's statue. They, like Daniel, knew the consequences of not following the king's order. They would be put to death. I find their response in verses 16-18 to be most audacious. Why would they answer the king in that manner? Why are we so surprised by their response?

4. Where did they get their internal spiritual conviction to answer the king as they did? Where does one get that type of conviction and how do you keep it?

5. Chapter 5 of this book lists four possibilities of where they received their conviction. What do you feel is the strongest way to attain that conviction? Within your group, discuss each of the four different possibilities and determine if there is one more important than the others.

6. This was a life and death trial that these three young men faced. What trials are you walking through as a leader right now? If none right now, please explain a recent trial. Do you have faith that the Lord can deliver you from those trials?

7. If the Almighty doesn't answer your prayers as you think they should be answered, where will you be in your faith walk? Will you become angry at God for being silent or for not answering your prayers? Will you turn your back on God as many have done in the past?

8. Read Proverbs 27:17. We must ask ourselves; how does one maintain that level of conviction? The answer is, by iron sharpening iron. Shadrach, Meshach, and Abednego were three friends that were iron sharpening iron. Do you have deep relationships like that? What will it take to get to that level of friendship?

9. List each of the six Leadership Life Principles in Chapter 5 of this book.

   A.

   B.

   C.

   D.

   E.

   F.

10. If you were going to write a whitepaper on one of the six Leadership Life Principles that spoke most to your heart, which one would it be? Why? Share with your group your thoughts on each of the Leadership Life Principles.

11. What three things did the Holy Spirit reveal to you about this lesson on men secure in their conviction?

    A.

    B.

    C.

12. Make a list of five items to help you in becoming more proficient in leading a life of conviction.

A.

B.

C.

D.

E.

WEEK 6
CALEB - A MAN OF COURAGE

1. Read Numbers 13:1-3, 17-33. In this lesson we study the man called Caleb—a man of courage. We first are introduced to Caleb in 13:6 where Caleb is listed as one of the twelve spies chosen to being a part of a recognizance mission to spy out the Promised Land. What kind of fruit did the spies bring back? What does this tell you about the land where the Lord was sending them?

2. They also reported to Moses about the people living in the land in 13:27-29 and 31-33. What did they report to Moses?

3. These twelve spies had also seen the ten plagues that God used to force Pharaoh to release them from bondage. They walked through the Red Sea with walls of water on each side of them and saw many other miracles. They had experienced the mighty hand of God in these miracles. What were they still afraid of and why?

4. Do you fear anything? If so, how can you overcome fear?

5. What does the Bible say about courage or being courageous? Joshua 1:7-9.

6. Read Numbers 13:30. Being courageous doesn't always mean you have no fear in a military confrontation. Speaking up when you hold a minority viewpoint on an issue can also cause fear. Caleb spoke up and tried to persuade the group that they could certainly take the land, even a land full of giants. Speaking up in front of a group can be frightening when things really matter, and you are in the minority. Have you ever had to speak up on a view that was not popular in front of a group? Did that cause you to fear? Were you subjected to pressure by the opposing side? Was your advice received well? What was the outcome?

7. Read Numbers 14:1-4. What does verse 4 say? What a great insult to the Lord who brought them out of captivity. Caleb, along with Joshua, again tried to silence the community by encouraging them that they could take the land, "Only do not rebel against the LORD" (Num 14:9). They were slaves in Egypt. Why would they even want to go back to Egypt?

8. Read Numbers 14:24. How does the Lord describe Caleb? How can this be applied to you?

9. We next see Caleb in Joshua 14:10-12. How do these verses describe Caleb forty-five years later? After all this time, where does his trust still lie?

10. By writing things out, we oftentimes have a better recollection of the material. Please list out the nine different Leadership Life Principles listed in this chapter.

A.

B.

C.

D.

E.

F.

G.

H.

I.

11. Which two of the nine Leadership Life Principles spoke to you the most? Why? Share with your group your thoughts on each of the Leadership Life Principles.

12. Leadership Life Principle #1: As a leader, dwell in the land of promises, not in the land of giants. What giants have you faced in past trials? You must learn to overcome any fear the enemy might send your way. How are you going to overcome that fear and be a man or woman of courage?

13. We often find ourselves in problems when we forget the great things God has done for us. As believers in Christ, we are all walking miracles. How can we keep reminding ourselves of the great things that God has done for us? Do you have a prayer journal where you can list these miracles in your life?

14. What three things did the Holy Spirit reveal to you about this lesson on being a person of courage?

A.

B.

C.

15. Make a list of five things you need to work on to become more a person of courage.

A.

B.

C.

D.

E.

WEEK 7
GIDEON - A MAN WHO LISTENED TO THE VOICE OF GOD

1. Read Romans 12:2. Most Christians want to hear from God and be touched by God in their daily walk but don't really know how to hear from God. Romans 12:2 is a good starting point. What does God want you to understand about renewing your mind? How does one get to the point of having a renewed mind?

2. Once you have grown to the point of having a renewed mind, the Bible says, "Then you will be able to test and *approve what God's will is*" (Rom 12:2, emphasis added). What does God want you to understand about renewing your mind?

3. The next logical step is to read and understand the Word of God. Through the reading of God's word, you can now determine the promptings from the Holy Spirit, that still small voice. Has the Spirit ever prompted you to say something, do something, or reach out to someone? Have you ever failed to do what was being asked? Why?

4. Do you listen to that still small voice or do you ignore it? Do you make excuses?

5. Do you become frustrated when you receive a prompting from the Spirit to do something because it conflicts with the busyness of the day and your daily tasks? How do you overcome your frustrations when the flesh collides with the spirit?

6. The angel showed up and addressed Gideon as a mighty warrior. What would you have thought or done if an angel showed up one day and called you a mighty warrior? The Holy Spirit had not been given to those of the Old Testament, therefore Gideon asked for physical signs. New Testament believers have the Holy Spirit to direct them. Should New Testament Christians be throwing out fleeces to determine the will of God? Please explain.

7. There are four different types of fear. 1. Fear of the Lord. 2. Fear of danger (for you or someone else) 3. Fear of the unknown. 4. Irrational fear. One and two are from God. Three and four are from the devil. Fear of the Lord is a good thing. Fear of danger—God built us to have this internal fear to alert us to danger and thus it is a good thing. Fear of the unknown is the place where ninety percent of our fear originates. This is based in our lack of faith and trust, therefore it is a sin issue. What would you do for the kingdom of God if you had no fear? If you could erase all internal fear from your thought life, what would you do? What would you be like?

8. Overcoming your fear so that you can hear from God requires you to build up your faith muscle. Have you ever been out on a limb? Have you ever been out on a limb so far that it begins to bend? What did you learn from this kind of faith builder? What was the outcome? What lessons did you learn that you could share with someone else walking through the same waters?

9. God will meet you in your fear, however that means that you need to initiate your step of faith. What does that look like for you? How do you begin to move forward when fear has you firmly in its grip?

10. If you want to walk on water, you need to get out of the boat. The boat is what is comfortable. The water and waves are the uncomfortable—the unknown. What is your boat? What needs to happen for you to get out of your boat?

11. Gideon was not equipped to lead an army. Where God calls, He equips. Do you believe that statement? How would He have to equip you for your next job assignment?

12. Leadership Life Principle #1 of Chapter 7 says, "Understand that God can use you in spite of your limitations." What are your perceived limitations? How might the Lord overcome those limitations?

13. What three things did the Holy Spirit reveal to you about this lesson on Gideon, a man who listened to the voice of God?

A.

B.

C.

14. Make a list of five things that need to occur to help you become more attentive to that still small voice.

A.

B.

C.

D.

E.

WEEK 8
JONATHAN - A MAN OF LOYALTY

1. How would you define loyalty? Share some examples from your life when loyalty was a positive experience. Do you have examples of when loyalty resulted in a negative experience?

2. Outside of your spouse, do you have close intimate friends with whom you can talk about anything? Are you loyal to one another?

3. How are you going to nurture relationships with friends, so they are as strong as the friendships of David and Jonathan or even Shadrach, Meshach, and Abednego? What needs to happen?

4. Is making friends hard for you? Please explain.

5. Have you ever been betrayed by a loyal friend? How does that feel? Did you reconcile? Do you think you will ever reconcile? How deep are the wounds?

6. How has the betrayal by a close, personal friend shaped your ability to have close relationships in the future?

7. Where does loyalty begin and where does it end? Loyalty starts with the seeds of trust between two individuals. As friendship and trust are developed over time, the level of loyalty grows. Should loyalty ever end? If it does have an ending, where is that point?

8. Regarding loyalty, when should you intervene if you see a friend moving down a path that would cause pain? Have you ever had to do that? What was the outcome? Did the friendship last?

9. To be in a loyal relationship understand two things: First, loyalty is a two-way street. Second, loyalty requires transparency. Have you ever been in a relationship where it seemed like loyalty was a one-way street? Have you ever been in a relationship where transparency was one-sided? What must happen for loyalty to flow both ways and for transparency to occur?

10. Why do people shy away from being transparent? Do you have an easy time or a hard time being transparent?

11. What three things did the Holy Spirit reveal to you about this lesson on loyalty?

   A.

   B.

   C.

12. Make a list of five things that need to occur to help you become a more loyal friend.

A.

B.

C.

D.

E.

WEEK 9
DAVID - A MAN OF STRATEGIC PLANNING

1. David could be described in many ways. In the context of this chapter we studied David as a strategic planner or a military strategist. Define what a strategic planner is. What is the job description of a strategic planner?

2. During the 2020 COVID-19 pandemic we saw major corporations struggle and go bankrupt. Many went bankrupt for several reasons. Two reasons were high debt and failure to forecast changing business trends. In other words, they failed to PIVOT. What does it mean to pivot? What does that mean in your organization, church or nonprofit? What does that mean in your personal life to pivot?

3. What does it mean to fail to pivot? What are the outcomes of failing to pivot?

4. You can have the strongest business plan but what happens when that plan collides with the will of God?

5. Although David can be viewed as a strategic planner, he also inquired of God in the direction that he should go. The Bible lists nine different occasions when David inquired of the Lord (1 Sam 23:1-3, 4-5, 10-11, 12-14, 30:8-9; 2 Sam 2:1-2, 5:17-21, 22-25, 21:1). He first had

a plan, inquired of the Lord, and then proceeded to take action. Most people leave off inquiring of the Lord, much to their demise. Please explain to your group an instance when you did not inquire of the Lord. How did that turn out for you? How can you get into the habit of inquiring of the Lord?

6. Read 2 Chronicles 32:1-5; 2 Kings 20:20. Hezekiah was a strategic thinker as well. He had built a tunnel underneath the city to bring water into the city. This tunnel can be toured in Jerusalem as a modern testament to the history recorded in the Old Testament. Have you ever thought of yourself as a strategic thinker? How can you, as a leader, become a more strategic thinker?

7. Read Proverbs 16:3: How does this verse help you understand what you should do when making plans?

8. Read Proverbs 19:21 What does this verse say about the Lord's purpose?

9. What three things did the Holy Spirit reveal to you about this lesson on becoming a strategic planner?

   A.

   B.

   C.

10. Make a list of five things that need to occur to assist you in becoming a better strategic thinker and planner.

A.

B.

C.

D.

E.

WEEK 10
ELEAZAR - A MAN WHO WOULD NOT RETREAT

1. Read 2 Samuel 23:8-10. These verses are the beginning of a narrative about the great exploits of David's mighty men. Verse 8 tells about the chief of the mighty men, Josheb-Basshebeth, who killed eight hundred men. Then we have the story of Eleazar, who was one of the three. Eleazar was a man who would not retreat. He stood his ground. Have you ever had to make a split-second military decision in the heat of battle? How did that go for you? If not in a military battle, what about the everyday world?

2. Have you ever had to stand your ground for a cause in which you strongly believed? Was it exhausting? Were you tired when you were done?

3. Why do you think the army around Eleazar retreated from the battle? Have you ever had people around you retreat in the heat of the battle? Why do some people retreat, and why do others stand their ground with you?

4. The Bible says he fought so hard that his hand froze to the sword. Can you imagine that he fought so hard, for so long and was so totally spent, that his hand had actually frozen to his sword? Have you ever fought so hard for something that you were totally spent at the end of the battle? What about at the end of each day?

5. Can you imagine what it was like attempting to pry his fingers from the sword? What must that have been like?

6. In Ephesians 6:17 the Bible says, "Take the helmet of salvation and the sword of the Spirit, which is the word of God." There is a connection to this New Testament verse, "the sword of the Spirit." What can you do in your daily life to tightly grab hold of the Word of God each day?

7. What causes people to stay in the battle so long that they are completely and totally spent? As a leader, what cause/s are you willing to take up with such fervor?

8. John Maxwell once said, "Everything rises and falls on leadership?" Do you agree or disagree with that statement? Please explain to the group.

9. Leadership Life Principle #1 of Chapter 10 says, "As a leader, stay the course when the going gets tough." What does it mean to stay the course?

10. If staying the course is so important, then why are so many pastors leaving the ministry each month? What could a pastor do to protect himself and his family from burnout?

11. As a leader, have your sword sharpened and ready for battle. Are you having regular, consistent, and fruitful quiet times? What does a quiet time do for your day? Can having a consistent quiet time protect you from the schemes of the devil?

12. What must you do to get in the habit of having a consistent quiet time?

13. What three things did the Holy Spirit reveal to you about this lesson on being a person who does not retreat?

    A.

    B.

    C.

14. Make a list of five tasks that need to occur to help you become a person who does not retreat from opposition.

    A.

    B.

    C.

    D.

    E.

WEEK 11
HEZEKIAH - A MAN WHO WORKED WHOLE-HEARTEDLY

1. Read 2 Kings 18:1-4. List all the points that you learned about King Hezekiah in this passage. What does this tell you about Hezekiah? His father, King Ahaz, was listed as an evil king in the Bible. How do you think Hezekiah, who becomes king at the age of twenty-five, turned out so different from his father?

2. What actions did he immediately take after becoming king?

3. Read 2 Kings 18:5-7. These verses add further meaning to our understanding of Hezekiah. List three things that pricked your heart about Hezekiah as described in these verses. What is the importance of verse 7?

4. Read 2 Chronicles 31:20-21. Between 2 Kings 18:1-7 and 2 Chronicles 31:20-21 five traits are highlighted below. These are all attributes to which we should all aspire. Which one do you have the most difficulty with and why?

   • Doing right in the eyes of the Lord
   • Trusted in the Lord
   • He held fast to the Lord

- Doing what was good, right, and faithful before the Lord
- Sought his God and worked wholeheartedly

5. Leadership Life Principle #1 in Chapter 11 says as leaders we are to "hold fast to the Lord!" What does that mean to you? Have you ever had difficulty in holding fast to the Lord? Please explain.

6. Colossians 3:23 says, "Whatever you do, work at it with all your heart, as working for the Lord, not for men." What does that mean to you? How does "working for the Lord" change your perspective when going to your earthly job? What areas might have to change in your work life to fully embrace this Scriptural principle?

7. Leadership Life Principle #2 of Chapter 11 states, "Leaders need to learn how to work wholeheartedly unto the Lord." Hezekiah worked wholeheartedly unto the Lord. Please give the group your definition of working wholeheartedly unto the Lord.

8. What do you think Hezekiah's core values were in life? What is a core value? Do you have core values for your personal life? Does your company have core values?

9. Leadership Life Principle #3 of Chapter 11 says, "A leader may need to initiate reforms." What is your definition of reform? Reform is another word for change.

Most people do not like change. Are you one of those people who does not like change? Are there areas in your work or personal life requiring reforms? Please list those reforms.

10. Do these reforms require other people to make changes as well? How will they react to your desire to make changes?

11. Leadership Life Principle #4 of Chapter 11 says that leaders need to learn to make the tough calls. Have you been able to make the tough calls in the past? Tough calls can be painful if other people's emotions and personalities are involved. Give an example of the last tough call you needed to make in either your personal or professional life. How did that go? Was it easy or difficult? Was there any fall out?

12. What three things did the Holy Spirit reveal to you about this lesson on working wholeheartedly?

    A.

    B.

    C.

13. Make a list of five things that need to occur for you to become better at working wholeheartedly unto the Lord.

A.

B.

C.

D.

E.

WEEK 12
PAUL - A MAN WHO GAVE IT HIS ALL

1. Read Acts 8:1, 3, Acts 9:1, Acts 22:3-5, Acts 26:5, Acts 26:9-11, Philippians 3:4-8. What do we know about Paul's life before his experience on the road to Damascus? What might cause so much hatred in a person? Do you see any correlation between the hatred in Paul's days and the hatred we see by some in our society today?

2. On his travels to Damascus, Paul has a conversion experience unlike any other listed in the New Testament. After being struck blind, he ended up at Judas' house on Straight Street for three days. The Bible says he neither ate nor drank. What do you think was going through Paul's mind during those three days? He was face to face with the fact that the beliefs that he held dear to him were wrong. What internal turmoil do you think he experienced in that time?

3. Paul went to Arabia where he stayed for three years. After Arabia, he went to Jerusalem via Damascus to meet with Peter. The Bible says he was with Peter for fifteen days. Peter had to have known about Paul's reputation. What do you think Peter thought when told Paul was waiting to see him?

4. After receiving the call to preach Jesus to the Gentiles, Paul had to sacrifice much over the course of his ministry. In the beginning, Paul found himself under immense suspicion by the Jews as well as the Christians. He suffered loss when the Jews, instead of loving him, began hating him. He lost all position within the Jewish community when he started preaching Jesus. He lost prestige, power, and respect. At one point, the Jews even took a vow that forty of them would not eat or drink anything until they had killed Paul (Acts 23:12-24). How might you have responded to this type of ongoing threat of bodily harm?

5. Leadership Life Lesson #1 of Chapter 12 says that we should understand that no one is outside of God's reach. We oftentimes pass judgment on the way someone looks. Sometimes we pass judgment on someone's reputation and think that person could never get saved. If there was ever a person one might think could never come to Jesus, it would be Paul. How would you react if some well-known "bad guy" showed up on your doorstep and told you that he had come to know Jesus? Would you believe him? Would you invite him into your house? Would you spend the next fifteen days with him?

6. Read 2 Corinthians 11:23-28. Can you feel the passion coming from Paul in these Scriptures? What most struck you about this passage? At what point would you have been tempted to quit?

7. Read Corinthians 12:9-10. Paul persevered. He ran the race marked out for him. He didn't quit. He didn't retire. Paul was a man who gave it his all. From where does this kind of inner strength come? How can this inner strength be maintained for the long haul, especially in times of continual stress, so that one does not become burned out in ministry?

8. How did Paul prevent all the attacks from penetrating his spiritual armor? What must you do to protect yourself when you come under attack?

9. What three things did the Holy Spirit reveal to you about the life of Paul?

A.

B.

C.

10. Make a list of five things that need to occur to assist you in giving it your all and not succumbing to burnout.

A.

B.

C.

D.

E.

BIBLIOGRAPHY

Books

Graham, Franklin. *Rebel with a Cause.* Nashville, TN: Thomas Nelson, 1997.

Web

Economy, Peter. "6 Keys to Getting Organized." Inc. Accessed August 12, 2020. https://www.inc.com/peter-economy/6-keys-to-getting-organized.html.

Hudson, Joshua. "Men of Valor." Poem Hunter. Accessed August 12, 2020. https://www.poemhunter.com/poem/men-of-valor/.

Schilling, David Russell. "Knowledge Doubling Every 12 Months, Soon to Be Every 12 Hours." Industry Tap. Accessed August 12, 2020. https://www.industrytap.com/knowledge-doubling-every-12-months-soon-to-be-every-12-hours/3950.

OTHER RESOURCES
Staving Off Disaster

A Journey in Spiritual Fasting

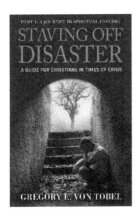

Got problems? I know you do. Kids are going sideways. Accidents happen. Relationships are strained. Houses are being foreclosed upon. Jobs are being lost. Brain tumors are being discovered. Car engines are blowing up. Identities are being stolen. Pornography can be accessed on smartphones. Hackers are hacking. Kids are overdosing. College women are being date-raped. Planes are going down. ISIS is on the move. New viruses are being discovered. Home invasions are happening. Children are bearing children. Fathers are leaving their posts. Kids are killing kids in schools. Christians are being martyred and imprisoned around the world for their faith. Sharia law is coming to the United States. The problems go on and on and on. It seems as if the wheels are coming off the world, and they are.

Christian believer, if you or someone you know is going through the fires of trials and tribulations, this book on biblical fasting is for you. Biblical fasting is a powerful spiritual tool virtually ignored by the Body of Christ today. Author Greg Von Tobel explains the correct motives for fasting, the wrong ways to fast, the biblical precedence for the church today to fast, and outlines ten steps to kick-starting your lifelong fasting discipline.

Biblical Leadership in Turbulent Times

Book One
Basic Leadership Principles for Christian Leaders

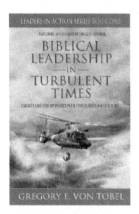

Have you ever met a great Christian leader whom you admire? You often marvel at what makes that person tick. You think to yourself, "Could I ever get to that level of being a Christian leader?"

How do leaders arrive at this point? Are they born that way? Or have they walked through a multitude of failures that have molded them into who they are today?

Mr. Von Tobel, in his recent book, Biblical Leadership in Turbulent Times, uses 1 Corinthians 13 as a backdrop to outline fourteen leadership traits for all levels of Christian maturity.

Travel with him as you learn biblical traits that will take your personal journey of leadership to the next level.

Prison Ministry Training

Part One
Getting Started in Prison Ministry

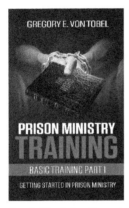

Modern-day prison ministry can feel like an uncertain and daunting path to navigate alone. Even for those who feel the calling, it can be a challenge to understand how best to begin.

Now, you can learn time-tested and proven methods from one of the world's most renowned experts in prison ministry. An unrivaled training guide, *Prison Ministry Training, Basic Training Part 1: Getting Started in Prison Ministry* is composed of multiple sections for the reader.

Unlike any other book on prison ministry, *Prison Ministry Training* is a completely innovative and contemporary approach to this ministry. With the tools learned, you will have the power to help individuals transform into people with newfound purpose in God's Kingdom.

Prison Ministry Training

Part Two
Volunteer Recruiting, Training, and Oversight

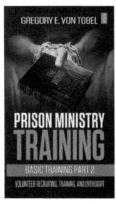

If you have ever worked with volunteers, you know leading volunteers can be like herding cats. Volunteers are often self-absorbed, marching to different drummers. The author, Gregory E. Von Tobel, having over thirty-five years of working with volunteers, shares his lessons learned. In this groundbreaking book, Mr. Von Tobel uses Exodus 18 as a backdrop to outline the best practices in running a volunteer organization, recruiting volunteers, as well as training and overseeing volunteers.

Now, you can learn time-tested and proven methods from one of the world's most renowned experts in prison ministry. An unrivaled training guide, *Prison Ministry Training, Part Two* is composed of multiple sections for the reader.

In this book you will learn: The hot potato approach to expanding a prison ministry, how and where to recruit volunteers, recruiting the younger generation, understanding the code of conduct for volunteers, and techniques in overcoming volunteer problems.

Prison Ministry Training

Part Three
Conducting An Effective Bible Study, Church Service, Altar Call, Prison Ministry Network, and Working with Staff

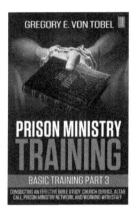

For those who are called to preach the Gospel of Jesus Christ in the jails and prisons, there isn't a great deal of instructive material available. Gregory E. Von Tobel has filled that void. In this third installment of *Prison Ministry Training*, he provides a step-by-step guide for pastors and lay leaders who are inspired to work with offenders. Von Tobel brings over three decades of experience to this concise yet detailed book.

He sketches out exactly how to conduct an effective church service in prison. For the crucial part of the service, the altar call, he maps out the best way to clearly and concisely present the Gospel. Once complete, you will understand:

- The seven steps to conducting an effective church service
- Preaching tips for the jail setting versus the prison setting
- The importance of doing an altar call
- The six different steps to giving an effective altar call
- The three distinctive styles of delivering an altar call
- Developing a state-wide prison ministry network
- The best ways of working with the staff of the institution

ABOUT THE AUTHOR

As a former stockbroker, Gregory E. Von Tobel has been involved in full-time prison missionary work for over thirty years. He is the founder and president of Prisoners For Christ Outreach Ministries (PFC), a ministry dedicated to taking the Gospel of Jesus Christ into the jails, prisons, and juvenile institutions not only in Washington State but also worldwide. PFC has field offices in eighteen foreign countries, including Burkina Faso, Burundi, Cameroon, Congo- DRC, Ethiopia, India, Kenya, Malawi, Nepal, Niger, Nigeria, Russia, Rwanda, Sierra Leonne, Tanzania, The Philippines, Togo, and Uganda.

PFC's volunteers worldwide conduct more than five hundred and ten church services and Bible studies per month, more than sixteen services per day. PFC's national Bible Study Correspondence School has over twenty-five hundred inmates on its student-body roster. Also, PFC's national inmate newspaper, *Yard Out*, is sent to over twelve hundred prison institutions nationally. In addition, PFC has over fifteen hundred volunteers in the ministry worldwide in some capacity, coming from over one-hundred different churches.

Mr. Von Tobel was a stockbroker for eleven years, from 1978 through 1989, for various firms, including EF Hutton & Co. and Shearson Lehman Brothers, when God called him into full-time prison ministry work. On May 14, 1990, God closed one chapter of his life, and on the following day, May 15, 1990, God opened up a whole new chapter. As of 1984, Greg has been ministering in Washington State jails and prisons, six years on a volunteer basis, and the last thirty years as a full-time missionary to those incarcerated.

Mr. Von Tobel has also served on the Governor's Panel of the Department of Corrections' Religious Services Advisory Council, assisting the department in setting religious policies and practices for inmates. In addition, he has served as past president of the Washington Chaplains Association and was a former Duvall City Councilman.

Greg has been married to Rhonda for the past forty-two years. They have three children and five grandchildren.

Made in USA - North Chelmsford, MA
1213109_9798698169352
12.15.2020 0841